535.078
Woo

122483
Wood, Robert W.

Light Fundamentals

LIGHT FUNDAMENTALS

Other books in the FUNdamental Series
Electricity and Magnetism FUNdamentals
Heat FUNdamentals
Mechanics FUNdamentals
Sound FUNdamentals

LIGHT

FUNDAMENTALS

FUNtastic Science Activities for Kids

Robert W. Wood

Illustrated by Steve Hoeft

Chelsea House Publishers

Philadelphia

Library of Congress Cataloging-in-Publication Data

Wood, Robert W., 1933-
      Light fundamentals : funtastic science activities for kids /
Robert W. Wood : illustrated by Steve Hoeft.
      p. cm — (FUNdamentals)
Originally published: New York : McGraw-Hill, 1996.
Includes index.
      Summary: Provides instructions for a variety of experiments
introducing the study of light, its characteristics, sources, and uses.
      ISBN 0-7910-4843-8 (hardcover)
      1. Light—Experiments—Juvenile literature. [. Light-
-Experiments. 2. Experiments.] I. Hoeft, Steve, ill. II. Title.
III. Series: FUNdamentals (Philadelphia, Pa.)
QC360.W66 1997b
535'.078—dc21   97-23975
                                                                    CIP
                                                                    AC

CONTENTS

INTRO

This is a book about light. Light is an amazing phenomenon that was once a great mystery. Many years ago, light was thought to be something that traveled from our eyes to the object we saw. We now know that light from another source is reflected from what we see to our eyes.

Light is something we all take for granted, but without it, we could not live. Light from the sun provides most of our energy and warmth. It allows us to see and allows plants to grow. Sunlight governs our daily lives—how we will dress, where we will go, and how we will spend our time.

Our most important light source is the sun. Before fire was discovered, our prehistoric ancestors could not see after the sun went down, making nighttime very scary. Early civilizations used flaming torches, then later developed oil lamps and candles. Gaslights were developed next. The incandescent lamp (a regular lightbulb) we use today has a thin, metal wire called a *filament*. The filament is heated to the glowing point by electricity.

Light is a form of *electromagnetic radiation*. This means that light is made up of things that are both electrical and magnetic in nature. There are

other forms of electromagnetic radiation such as radio waves, television waves, radar waves, microwaves, and X-rays. But light is the only one we can see.

Today, many forms of energy are turned into light. These advances allow hospitals, factories, and transportation systems to operate around the clock. The study of light is also responsible for dramatic advances in electronics and has allowed us to build more powerful microscopes and telescopes, which help us to better understand the universe around us.

The experiments in this book are a basic introduction to the study of light. You'll learn what light is, where it comes from, and some of the ways you can use it. Each experiment begins with a challenge, followed by a materials list and step-by-step procedures. Results are given to explain what is being demonstrated, as well as a few questions to discuss further. Each experiment ends with fun facts.

Where measurements are used, they are given in both the English and metric systems as numbers that will make the experiments easy to perform. Use whichever system you like, but realize that the numbers might not be exact equivalents.

Be sure to read the Safety Stuff section before you begin any experiment. It recommends safety precautions you should take. It also tells you whether you should have a teacher or another adult help you. Keep safety in mind, and you are sure to have a rewarding first experience in the fascinating world of light.

SAFETY STUFF

Science experiments can be fun and exciting, but safety should always be considered. Parents and teachers are encouraged to participate with their children and students.

 Look over the steps before beginning any experiment. You will notice that some steps are preceded by a caution symbol like the one next to this paragraph. This symbol means that you should use extra safety precautions or that the experiment requires adult supervision.

Materials or tools used in some experiments could be dangerous in young hands. Adult supervision is recommended whenever the caution symbol appears. Children need to be taught about the care and handling of sharp tools or combustible or toxic materials and how to protect surfaces. Also, extreme caution must be exercised around any open flame or very hot surface.

Use common sense and make safety the priority, and you will have a safe and fun experience!

An optical illusion is
the mind playing tricks on the eye.

YIKES!
THERE'S A HOLE
IN MY HAND!

YOUR CHALLENGE

To create and observe an optical illusion.

DO THIS

1 Keeping both eyes open, place the tube in front of one eye
   like a telescope and look at a distant object. (Figure 1-1)

Look
through the
tube at a
distant object.

Scope this out!

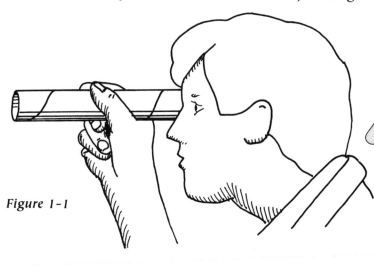

Figure 1-1

YOU NEED

**Empty paper-towel
cardboard tube
or rolled-up sheet
of paper**

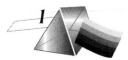

1

2 Bring the palm of your free hand up next to the tube so that the side of your hand is resting against the side of the tube. (Figure 1-2)

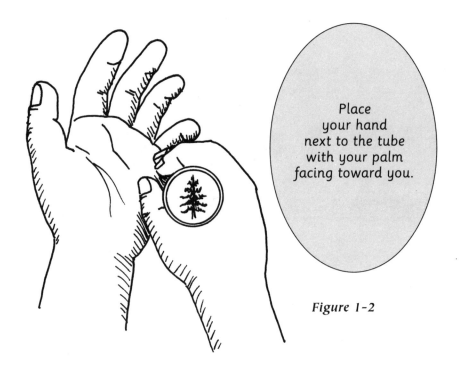

Place your hand next to the tube with your palm facing toward you.

Figure 1-2

WHAT HAPPENED?

A "hole" will appear, allowing you to see the distant object through your hand. This optical illusion occurs because our eyes see two images that are combined by our brain. In this case, one eye sees the distant object and the other sees the hand. These two images are combined by the brain to create the illusion.

Our minds can be tricked by the things we see. There are several kinds of illusions, but they all have something in common: the ability to make you see something that *is not* there or to *not* see something that *is* there. Is camouflage a form of an illusion? What animals can you think of that use camouflage for protection? What color is a chameleon?

Which kid is the tallest in the illustration? (Figure 1-3)

Which kid
is the tallest?

Here's a hint: You
might need a ruler
to get this one right!

Figure 1-3

GUESS WHAT?

⭐ Because of an optical illusion, a person wearing vertical stripes will look thinner than if the stripes were horizontal.

⭐ A white house will appear larger than the same house painted a darker color.

Did you know that our brains
act kind of like cameras?
Read on!

Now You See It...
Now You See It
Again

Your Challenge

To understand that our brain holds on to images for a few
seconds after the image is gone.

Do This

1   In a dark room, turn on the lamp and stare at the
    lightbulb for about 10 seconds. You should be several feet
    from the lamp. (Figure 2-1)

2   Switch off the lamp.

What Happened?

You will continue to see the lighted bulb. Your mind
continues to see an object for about one-tenth of a second
after the object is no longer visible. This means that if you
are shown 10 or more still pictures a second, your mind will
see them as an image in motion.

You Need

**Lamp with the shade
removed**

Darkened room

5

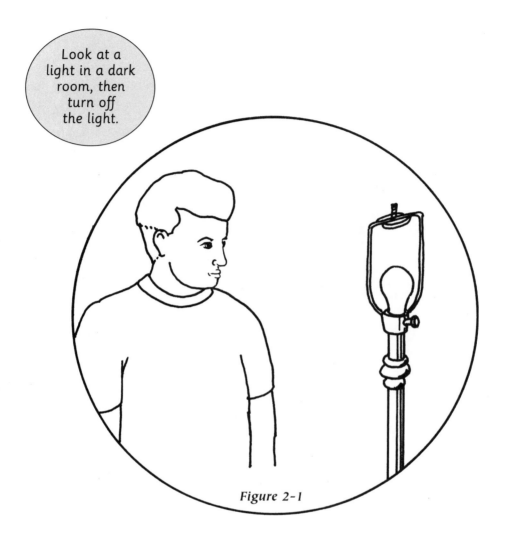

Look at a light in a dark room, then turn off the light.

Figure 2-1

This ability allows us to see the motion in pictures taken by movie and television cameras. Scenes captured on film are made up of a series of still pictures that are set in motion.

How many times a day do you see pictures in motion? How many ways can you think of that science uses motion pictures to study objects? What is time-lapse photography? How can it be used to study plants or soil erosion? How can motion pictures be used to study lightning?

GUESS WHAT?

★ Ultra-high-speed cameras can record events that happen too fast for us to see. For example, they can have exposures as brief as one-millionth of a second and can "freeze" a bullet traveling at 15,000 miles per hour (24,000 km per hour).

★ Unlike most animals, we depend primarily on sight to know our surroundings. Because our early ancestors could only see by the light from the sun, nighttime was dangerous. One of the most important advances occurred when humans learned to control fire, a source of light. Torches, candles, and oil lamps use chemical reaction—burning—to produce energy that we see as light.

★ Glowworms, fireflies, and some plants use chemical energy to produce energy. They are called bioluminescent. Lightbulbs and neon lights use electricity to produce light.

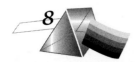

> Shed a little light
> on the subject!

I SEE RIGHT THROUGH YOU

YOUR CHALLENGE

To observe how different materials affect light rays.

DO THIS

1 Place a flashlight on a stack of books and turn the flashlight ON.

2 Hold the clear plastic in front of the flashlight and see how much light passes through it. (Figure 3-1)

3 Repeat Step 2 with each of the different materials.

WHAT HAPPENED?

The clear plastic is *transparent*, and light can pass through transparent materials. Images can be seen clearly through

YOU NEED

Flashlight

Stack of books

Sheet of clear plastic such as food wrap

Sheet of waxed paper

Piece of cardboard

9

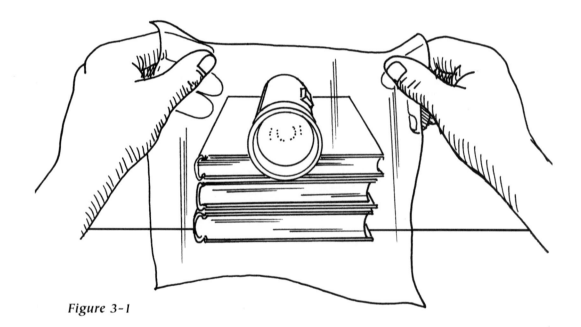

The clear plastic
allows light to
pass through without
being scattered.

Figure 3-1

transparent materials such as window panes. The sheet of waxed paper
is *translucent*. Some light did pass through the translucent material, but
most of the light was scattered. Images cannot be seen clearly through
translucent material. Frosted glass is a translucent material. (Figure 3-2)

The cardboard is *opaque*. Light cannot pass through opaque material. Opaque materials absorb and reflect light. Aluminum foil is an opaque material.

Are sunglasses made of transparent, translucent, or opaque material? What type of material would you expect filters for cameras to be made of? How would you compare light passing through a transparent cover with a translucent one? Which one produces the softest light? Which light would be better for reading?

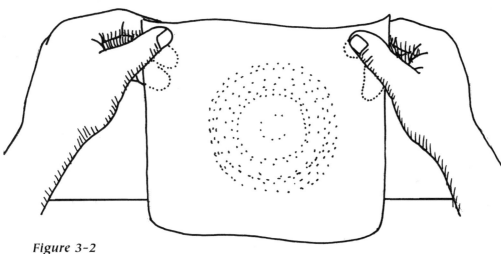

Figure 3-2

Wax paper scatters most of the light.

GUESS WHAT?

⭐ Several kinds of fish called glassfish have transparent bodies that allow part of the skeleton and some of the internal organs to be clearly seen. They are from 2 to 4 inches (5 to 10 cm) long and live in southern Asia. Certain species of glassfish are also popular in home aquariums.

⭐ Lantern fish comprise about 200 species of small fish with light organs along their sides. They are about 6 inches (15 cm) long and live deep in the ocean. (Figure 3-3)

⭐ One of the most bizarre frogs in the world is the centrolene frog found in Central America. It has green bones covered with translucent skin.

Lantern fish live in the mid-depths of the ocean, down to about 3,000 feet, or 1 kilometer.

Figure 3-3

Let me bounce this one off of you!

REFLECTING ON REFLECTING

YOUR CHALLENGE

To compare how different materials reflect light.

DO THIS

1 Place the books binding-to-binding to support the mirror and a white card. Prop the mirror against one of the books. Then prop a white card against the other book.

2 Turn out the lights. Position the flashlight so that the beam hits the mirror and bounces onto the card. Notice the brightness of the light on the card. (Figure 4-1)

3 Now replace the mirror with the other white card and repeat the steps. Is the reflected light on the card as bright? (Figure 4-2)

4 Next, replace one of the white cards with a black card. Bounce the beam off the black card and onto the white

YOU NEED

Darkened room

Two large books

Small, flat mirror

Two white cards

Flashlight

Dull black card

13

card. Compare the amount of light reflected from the three different materials. (Figure 4-3)

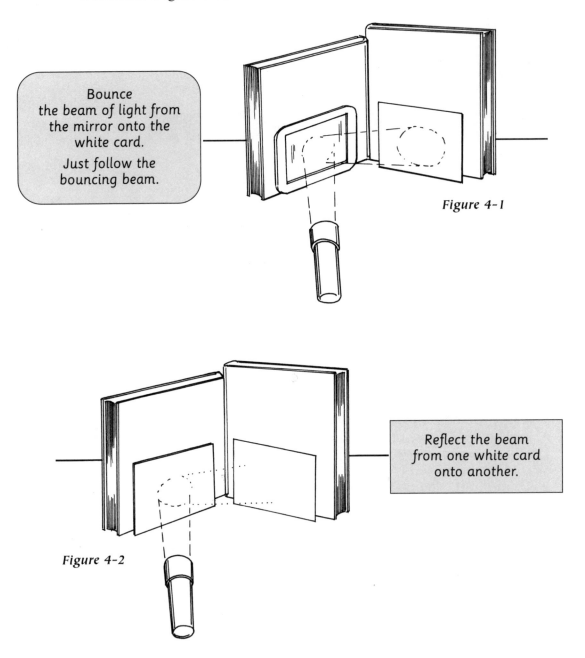

Bounce the beam of light from the mirror onto the white card.

Just follow the bouncing beam.

Figure 4-1

Reflect the beam from one white card onto another.

Figure 4-2

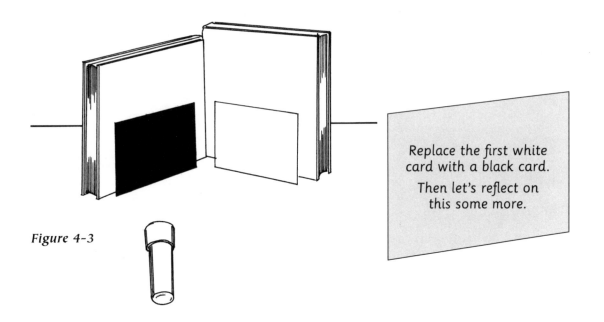

Figure 4-3

Replace the first white card with a black card.

Then let's reflect on this some more.

WHAT HAPPENED ?

The mirror reflected almost all of the light from the flashlight. The white card reflected some light but not as much as the mirror. The black card reflected very little light.

Without light we could see nothing at all. Unlike the sun, very few objects give off any light of their own. We are able to see these objects only because of the light reflected from them. You are able to see this page because of the light reflected from it.

The amount of light reflected from an object depends on the surface of the object. The mirror has a smooth, shiny surface. The light strikes this surface in a certain pattern, then it is reflected in the same pattern. The darker and duller the material, the more light it absorbs and the less light it reflects.

15

Why do some ball players wear black ointment under their eyes? If a dark material absorbs light, will it become warmer? What color clothing would you choose to wear in the desert? How about in the Arctic? At night, would a black car be cooler to the touch than a white car? How could colors be used to generate heat or cold?

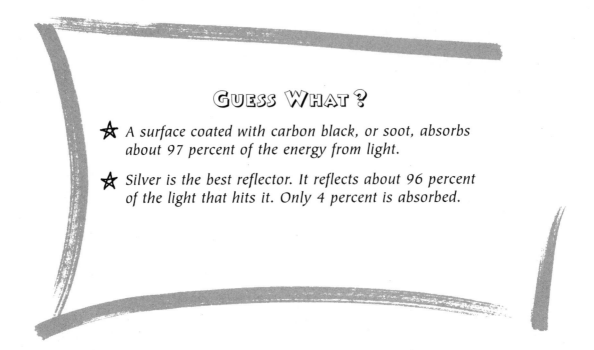

Guess What?

⭐ *A surface coated with carbon black, or soot, absorbs about 97 percent of the energy from light.*

⭐ *Silver is the best reflector. It reflects about 96 percent of the light that hits it. Only 4 percent is absorbed.*

Can you see yourself as others see you?

INSPECTING REFLECTING

YOUR CHALLENGE

To observe how light rays reflect images from a mirror.

DO THIS

1   Look into a mirror. (Figure 5-1)

2   Study the image you see. For all practical purposes, the image you see will be yourself.

WHAT HAPPENED?

The image you see is not the "real" you. Although light rays *seem* to come from the image in the mirror, they actually come from you and travel to your eye by reflection from the surface of the mirror. What you see is a *reflection* of your image.

We often think that a mirror reverses your image, but actually it doesn't. When you stand in front of a full-length mirror,

YOU NEED

Mirror

17

> Look closely
> at the image
> in the mirror.

Figure 5-1

your left foot will appear on your left in the mirror and you will also appear right-side up. We tend to think of the image in the mirror as an object instead of a reflection. If it were an object, it would be reversed.

As you back away from the mirror, your image appears smaller. This is because the image is as large as you would appear to be if someone else saw you at the same distance.

Because of the viewing angle, if you can see someone else in a mirror, he or she also can see you in that mirror. The only exception is if you are in the dark where there is no light to be reflected.

If you were in a car following a large truck and you could not see the truck driver in the truck's mirrors, would the truck driver know you were there? Could this be dangerous? Could mirrors be used to send messages? Do you think a pilot in an airplane could see sunlight reflected from a small pocket mirror on the ground?

GUESS WHAT?

★ *If you are 3 feet (1 m) in front of a mirror, your reflection appears the same as if it were 3 feet behind the mirror.*

★ *In ancient times, superstitious people believed that they could lose their souls to a mirror.*

★ *In Greek mythology, the hideous Medusa could be looked at only through a mirror; otherwise, the beholder would turn to stone.*

There are always
two or more ways
of looking at things!

FLIP SIDE

YOUR CHALLENGE

To reverse a mirror image and see how we actually appear to others.

DO THIS

1. Tape the two mirrors together so that they will stand upright and form an angle of about 45 degrees. (Figure 6-1)

2. Place the clock so that it faces the two mirrors, and read the numbers. They will be in the correct order. (Figure 6-2)

3. Place a page of a book in front of the mirror. Try reading the page of a book. You will see that you can.

4. Now look in the mirrors and try to comb your hair. This might be confusing!

YOU NEED

Two pocket mirrors

Transparent tape

Small tabletop clock

Book page

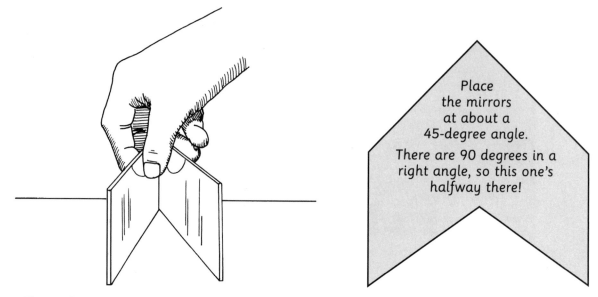

Place the mirrors at about a 45-degree angle.

There are 90 degrees in a right angle, so this one's halfway there!

Figure 6-1

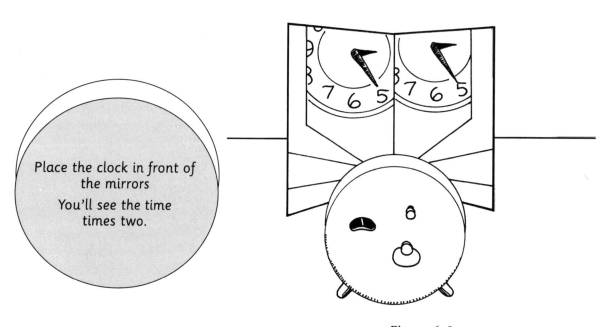

Place the clock in front of the mirrors

You'll see the time times two.

Figure 6-2

22

WHAT HAPPENED?

Light traveling from the left side of your face travels to the left mirror, which is reflected to the right mirror and then back again to your eye. Light traveling from the right side makes the same trip in reverse and is reflected back from the mirror on the left. This is the way you appear to others, instead of the way you see yourself in the mirror. This is an image opposite to the one from a single mirror. (Figure 6-3)

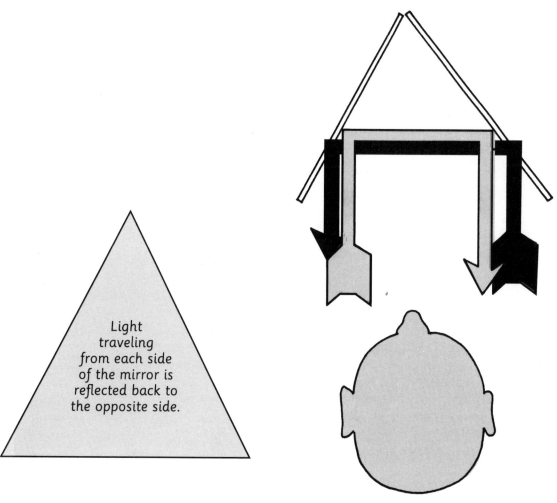

Light traveling from each side of the mirror is reflected back to the opposite side.

Figure 6-3

23

Can you write your name while holding the paper up in front of a mirror? Must a dentist reverse the direction of movements while working with a mirror? Stand in front of a mirror while holding another mirror. How many images can you see? Move the mirror in your hand. What happens to the images?

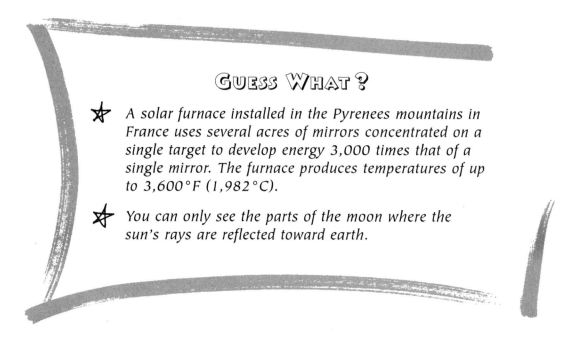

GUESS WHAT ?

★ *A solar furnace installed in the Pyrenees mountains in France uses several acres of mirrors concentrated on a single target to develop energy 3,000 times that of a single mirror. The furnace produces temperatures of up to 3,600°F (1,982°C).*

★ *You can only see the parts of the moon where the sun's rays are reflected toward earth.*

Don't get bent out of shape!
Just reflect on this experiment.

LOONY SPOONS

YOUR CHALLENGE

To distort an image by reflecting light on a curved surface.

DO THIS

1 Look at your reflection in the back of a shiny spoon. (Figure 7-1)

YOU NEED

Large, shiny spoon

The image from the back of the spoon.

Figure 7-1

2   Now look at your reflection in the front of the spoon. (Figure 7-2)

The image
from the
front of
the spoon
is inverted.

You're
upside
down!

Figure 7-2

3   Compare the images.

WHAT HAPPENED?

The back of the spoon, which curves outward, produces a smaller image. The front of the spoon, which curves inward, produces a larger image. The image is also upside down because the light from the top of your head is reflected from the bottom of the spoon, and the light from the bottom of your head is reflected from the top of the spoon.

Mirrors that curve outward are called *convex* mirrors. They are often used as sideview mirrors on cars because light is reflected from a wide area behind the car. This produces a smaller image but gives the driver a wider field of vision.

The mirrors that curve inward are called *concave* mirrors. They are found in homes and are used as shaving and makeup mirrors. The curve is very slight, so the image is not inverted, or upside down. Large concave mirrors are also used to make powerful reflecting telescopes. (Figure 7-3)

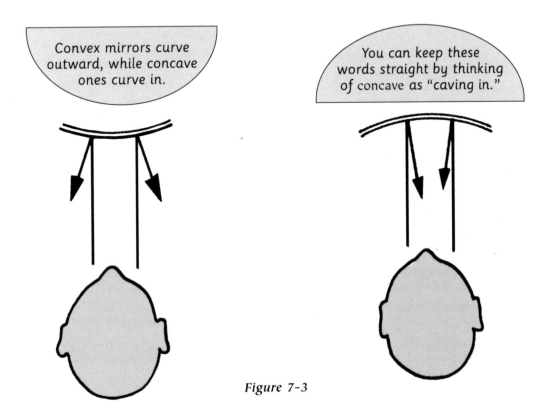

Figure 7-3

The wavy mirrors that you find in fun houses at fairs and amusement parks are partly convex and partly concave. They produce both narrow and wide images on the same mirror.

Would large convex mirrors be a safety feature at the intersection of hallways? Why would convex mirrors be useful near the doors of an elevator? What type of mirror would you expect to find near the ceiling of a store?

GUESS WHAT?

★ One of the problems with building extra-large telescopes is that the mirrors can be distorted because they could bend under their own weight.

★ A beam of light is invisible unless it strikes an eye or a surface or particles that reflect parts of the beam to the eye.

It's a magic marble multiplier!

MIRROR MULTIPLICATIONS

YOUR CHALLENGE

To observe images that are reflected several times.

DO THIS

1 Place the books about 1 foot (30.48 cm) apart on a table. Position the books so that the edges of the pages face each other. These will be the supports for the mirrors.

2 Partly raise one of the covers and stand a mirror upright against the edge of the pages. Rest the cover on the top of the mirror to hold it in place. Repeat the steps with the other mirror so that you have two mirrors facing each other. (Figure 8-1)

3 Place the marble on the spool and set it an equal distance between the mirrors. Look just above one mirror into the other. (You might need to adjust the angle of the mirrors a little.) (Figure 8-2)

YOU NEED

Two hardback books

Two pocket mirrors

Marble

Spool from sewing thread

29

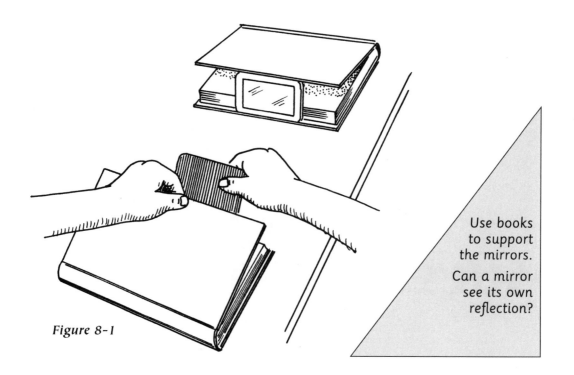

Figure 8-1

Use books to support the mirrors.

Can a mirror see its own reflection?

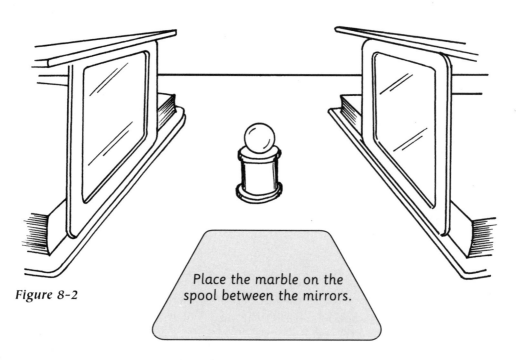

Figure 8-2

Place the marble on the spool between the mirrors.

WHAT HAPPENED?

When both mirrors are properly aimed, you will be able to see a number of marbles, gradually getting smaller and disappearing into the mirror. (Figure 8-3)

The light from the marble causes its image to be reflected back and forth many times. The distance the reflection travels increases, so the image becomes smaller. As the images are reflected, they also become dimmer. This is because a little of the light energy is consumed during each reflection.

Would walking through a maze of mirrors be confusing? How are mirrors used to make rooms seem larger? How large would a room appear if two opposite walls were completely covered with mirrors?

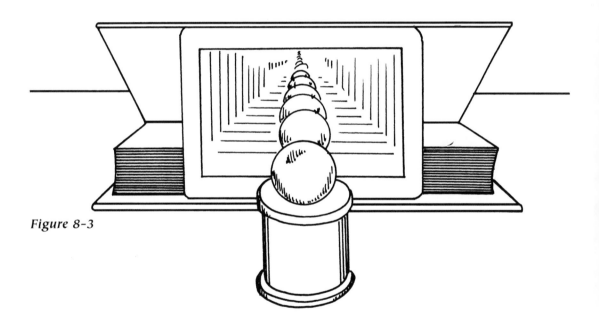

Figure 8-3

The mirrors multiply
the reflection.

How many marbles
do you see?

GUESS WHAT?

★ In a single-lens reflex (SLR) camera, the image is reflected by a mirror to the viewfinder. The mirror is located between the lens and the film. Just before the shutter opens, the mirror swings up out of the way. When the film is advanced for the next picture, the mirror is returned to the focusing position.

★ Because of the problems of building a very large single mirror, in 1978 a multi-mirror telescope in Arizona was built to use six mirrors that focused together. The mirrors acted like one mirror 21 feet (6 m) in diameter.

What goes in,
must go out—at the same angle!

STREAMS OF BEAMS

YOUR CHALLENGE

To observe that the angle in which light strikes a mirror is always the same angle as the light reflected.

DO THIS

1   Place the paper on a flat surface in the sunlight. Hold the comb with the teeth down on the paper. Position it so that the sunlight causes beams of light from the comb to fall across the paper. (Figure 9-1)

2   Place the mirror diagonally in the path of these beams. The beams will be reflected at an angle toward the edge of the paper. Notice the angle by which the beams strike the mirror and the angle by which they are reflected. Turn the mirror to different angles and notice the reflected beams. (Figure 9-2)

YOU NEED

Sheet of white paper

Comb

Bright sunlight

Mirror

Clear glass of water

33

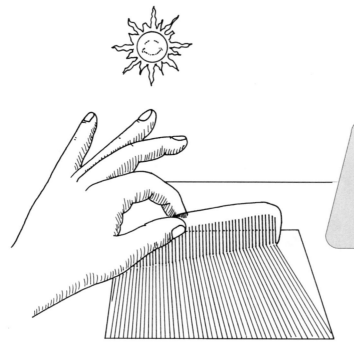

Place the comb so that the light rays fall across the paper.

Instead of splitting hairs, you're splitting sunshine!

Figure 9-1

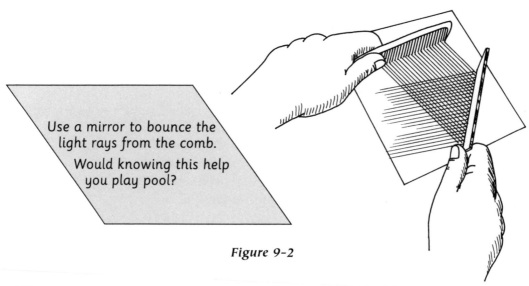

Use a mirror to bounce the light rays from the comb.

Would knowing this help you play pool?

Figure 9-2

34

3   Place a clear glass of water about 1 inch (2.5 cm) in front of the comb. What happens to the beams now?

WHAT HAPPENED ?

Light is reflected from a mirror at exactly the same angle it strikes the mirror. When the angle of the mirror is changed, the reflected beams change to the same angle. The angle at which light strikes the mirror is called the *angle of incidence*. The angle at which light is reflected is called the *angle of reflection*. Therefore, the angle of incidence is always equal to the angle of reflection.

Sideview mirrors on newer cars are designed so that the driver can see whatever is behind him or her at a wider angle. Why do sideview mirrors caution that "objects in mirror are closer than they appear"?

When light bounces from a mirror, is any force being applied to the mirror? If so, could this slight force be used to push a spaceship? Can you imagine a spaceship with sails made of mirrors? How does this form of travel compare with sailboats and the wind?

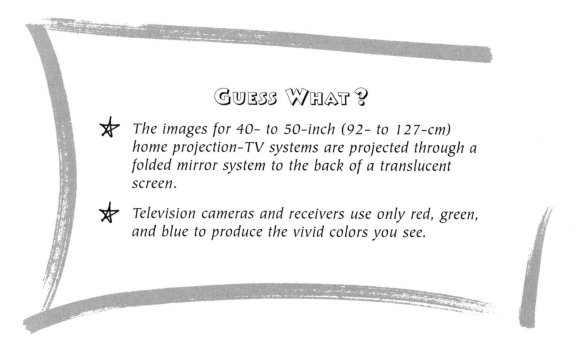

GUESS WHAT ?

⭐ *The images for 40- to 50-inch (92- to 127-cm) home projection-TV systems are projected through a folded mirror system to the back of a translucent screen.*

⭐ *Television cameras and receivers use only red, green, and blue to produce the vivid colors you see.*

Mirror, mirror on the wall,
let's measure where
the light beam falls!

REFLECTION CONNECTION

YOUR CHALLENGE

To compare the angle with which light strikes a mirror and angle of reflection.

DO THIS

1 Draw a dotted line down the center of the paper for a reference line. (Figure 10-1)

2 Draw a solid line at any angle from the dotted line. (Figure 10-2)

3 Place the mirror upright at the point where the straight line and the dotted line meet. Move the mirror, and line up the dotted line with its reflection in the mirror. (Figure 10-3)

4 Looking into the mirror, line up the edge of the ruler on the paper with the reflection of the straight line. Trace this line. (Figure 10-4)

YOU NEED

Pencil

Sheet of paper

Ruler

Mirror

Protractor

37

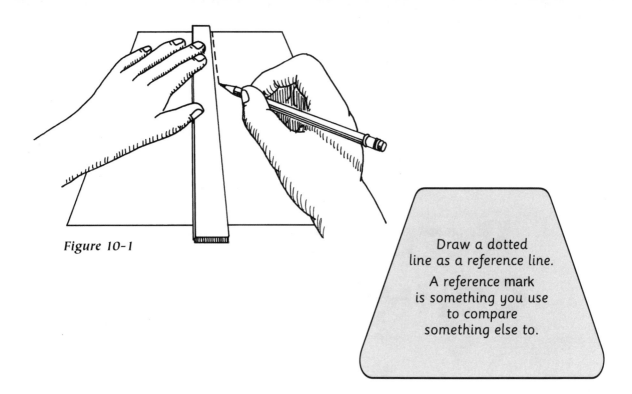

Figure 10-1

Draw a dotted line as a reference line.

A reference mark is something you use to compare something else to.

Draw a solid line across the reference line.

You don't need to draw the line to the edge of the paper.

Figure 10-2

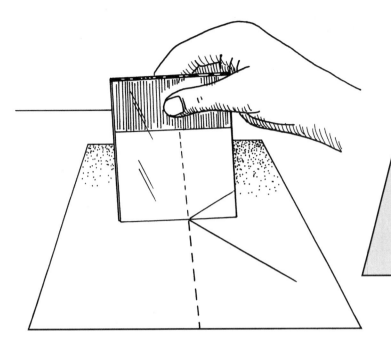

Figure 10-3

Place the mirror where the lines cross and line up the dotted reference line in the mirror.

Make sure the dotted line and its reflection are straight.

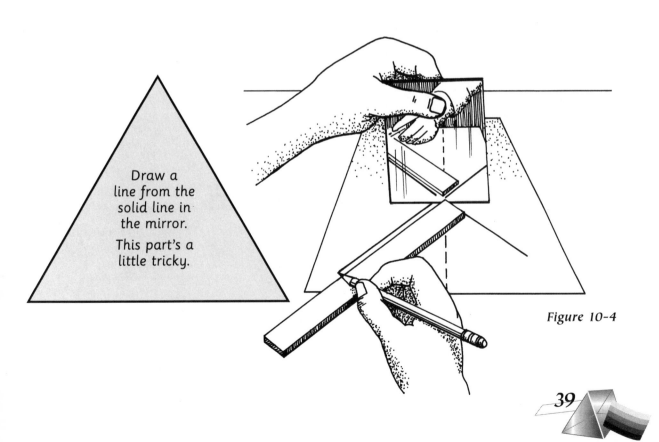

Draw a line from the solid line in the mirror.

This part's a little tricky.

Figure 10-4

39

5 Using a protractor, compare the angles of each straight line with the dotted line. (Figure 10-5)

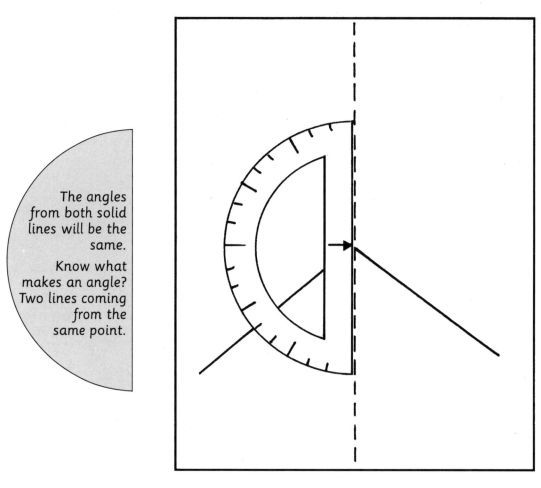

The angles from both solid lines will be the same.

Know what makes an angle? Two lines coming from the same point.

Figure 10-5

6 Repeat the experiment using different angles.

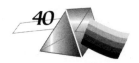

What Happened?

The protractor should show that light is reflected at the same angle it strikes the reflecting surface. The angle at which light strikes the mirror is called the *angle of incidence*. The angle at which it reflects from the mirror is called the *angle of reflection*.

How could mirrors be used to measure precise angles or the height of tall objects? How can mirrors be used to measure long distances? Could knowing about the angle of incidence and the angle of reflection help you play a game of pool?

Guess What?

★ The Hubble space telescope, launched in 1990, could not focus properly because of a faulty mirror. Fortunately, astronauts repaired it in 1993.

★ The Hubble telescope is expected to pick up and magnify light from about 20 billion light-years away. (A light-year *is the distance light travels in one year.*)

You'll be able to see what's just around the corner!

OUTTA SIGHT—NOT!

YOUR CHALLENGE

To construct and use a periscope.

DO THIS

1   Carefully cut the top from the carton (or have an adult do it). Then cut a rectangular opening in one side of the box near the top. (Never cut with an object held against yourself. You could slip and seriously injure yourself.) (Figure 11-1)

2   Cut another rectangular opening on the opposite side about the same distance from the bottom. (Figure 11-2)

3   Place the mirror faceup in the bottom of the carton at a 45-degree angle from the bottom opening. Tape the mirror in place. (Figure 11-3)

YOU NEED

One 1-quart (1 liter) milk carton or similar-size box

Utility knife

Two pocket mirrors

Transparent tape or masking tape

43

Figure 11-1

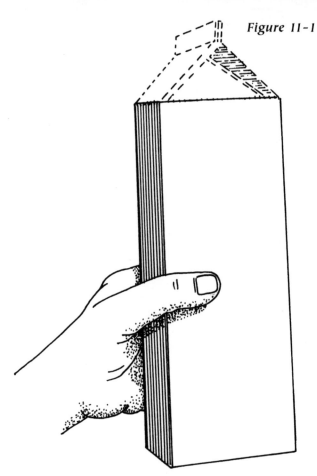

Cut the top from an empty milk carton.

Cut openings on opposite sides near the top and bottom of the carton.

The top opening should be the same distance from the top as the bottom opening is from the bottom.

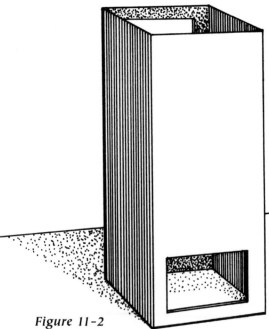

Figure 11-2

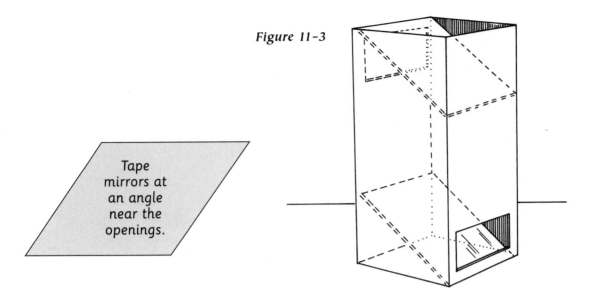

Figure 11-3

Tape mirrors at an angle near the openings.

4 Mount the upper mirror facedown at a 45-degree angle to the top opening. Tape this mirror in place. (Figure 11-4)

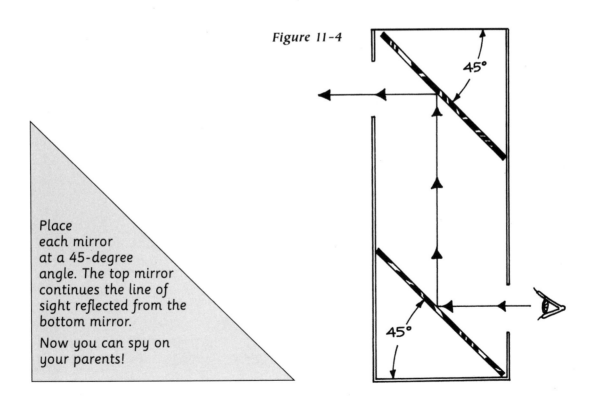

Figure 11-4

45°

45°

Place each mirror at a 45-degree angle. The top mirror continues the line of sight reflected from the bottom mirror.

Now you can spy on your parents!

5 Hold the periscope-carton so that the top opening is just past the corner of a wall and look into the bottom opening.

WHAT HAPPENED?

You should be able to see around the corner. Light travels from the object to the top mirror and is reflected down to the bottom mirror. Then the light is reflected to your eye.

We all know that submarines are equipped with periscopes to let people in them see above the water, but what other ways could we use them? Would periscopes be useful in checking drainage pipes? How could periscopes be used when dealing with hazardous waste?

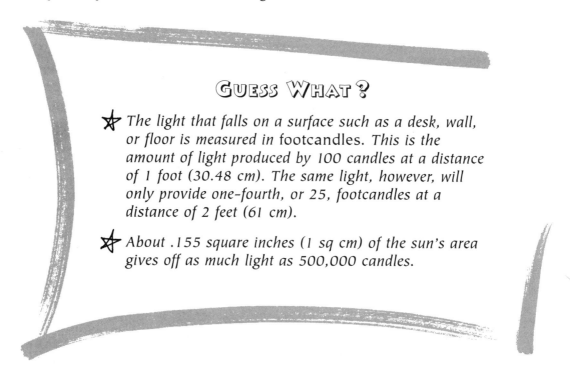

GUESS WHAT?

★ The light that falls on a surface such as a desk, wall, or floor is measured in footcandles. This is the amount of light produced by 100 candles at a distance of 1 foot (30.48 cm). The same light, however, will only provide one-fourth, or 25, footcandles at a distance of 2 feet (61 cm).

★ About .155 square inches (1 sq cm) of the sun's area gives off as much light as 500,000 candles.

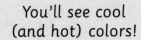

You'll *see cool* (and hot) colors!

BLACK TOMATOES?

YOUR CHALLENGE

To discover that the color of an object depends on the color of the light reflected to our eyes.

DO THIS

1   Fill the pan with about 1 inch (2.54 cm) of water and place it in bright sunlight. Place the mirror in the water and lean it so that it faces the sun at about 45 degrees.

2   Hold a sheet of white paper so that it catches the reflected beam. Some adjusting might be necessary, but you should see a rainbow of colors.

 3   Now cut each sheet of plastic into four equal pieces. (After cutting, you should have 12 pieces total.) (Figure 12-1)

YOU NEED

Bright, sunny day

Square pan

Water

Small mirror

White sheet of paper

Red, green, and blue sheets of plastic or cellophane

Scissors

Red and green objects about the same shades as the plastic (tomato, cucumber, etc.)

Flashlight

White wall

47

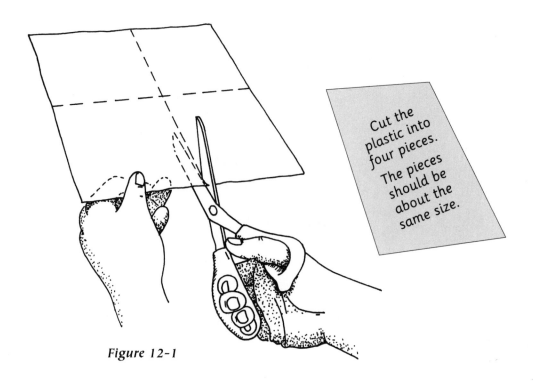

Cut the plastic into four pieces. The pieces should be about the same size.

Figure 12-1

4 Place the red and green objects side by side.

5 Shine the flashlight on the objects, and look at them through one sheet of red plastic. Add a second sheet of red plastic, then a third and fourth. (Figure 12-2)

6 Now look at the same objects through the green plastic. Add more layers of green plastic as you did with the red sheets. Did the objects change color?

7 Hold the red plastic in one hand and use the mirror to reflect a beam of sunlight through it and onto the wall. Repeat the steps with the green and blue sheets. (Figure 12-3)

8 Next, put the red, green, and blue sheets together and shine the sunlight beam through all three. What color was reflected on the wall?

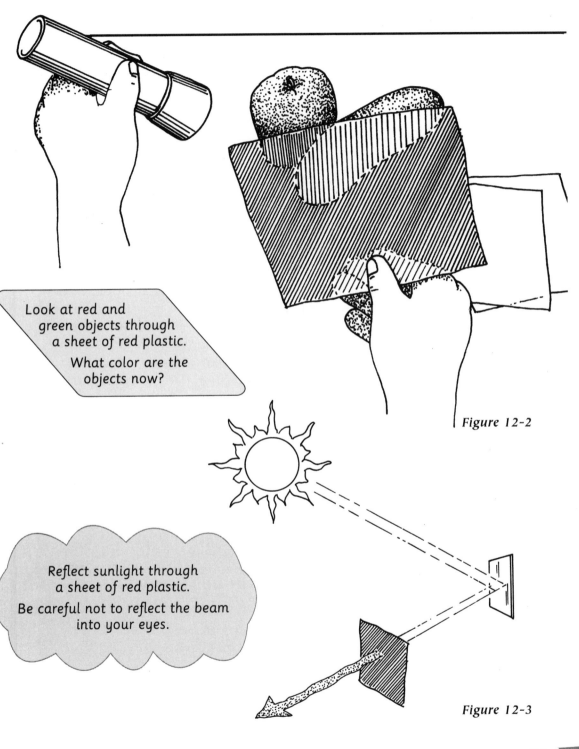

Look at red and
green objects through
a sheet of red plastic.

What color are the
objects now?

Figure 12-2

Reflect sunlight through
a sheet of red plastic.
Be careful not to reflect the beam
into your eyes.

Figure 12-3

49

WHAT HAPPENED?

Sunlight reflected through the bowl of water produced a spectrum of colors. These are the colors that make up white light.

When you used the flashlight and looked through the red plastic, the red object turned lighter. As more layers of red plastic were added, the object eventually turned white. (In fact, red printing on white paper will disappear.) The green object, on the other hand, became darker and turned black.

When the objects were viewed through the green plastic, the results were the opposite. The green object became lighter, and the red object darkened and turned black.

In normal light, a red object looks red because it absorbs all of the colors of the spectrum except red, which it reflects. When the light from the red object reached your eyes through the red plastic, the red was blocked and the object appeared black. Black is the absence of all color. Each sheet of colored plastic filters that particular color of light in the spectrum. Green plastic filters the green part, blue filters the blue part, and so on.

When you reflected sunlight through the red, green, and blue sheets, the colors combined to produce white light. For this reason, red, green, and blue are called *primary colors*. It was necessary to use sunlight because most flashlights do not produce a strong enough beam to go through the added sheets of colored plastic.

Why do photographers use a red safelight in darkrooms? How are different-colored lights used to provide information? What does a red or green light usually mean? What colors of lights would you expect to find at an airport? At a harbor?

GUESS WHAT?

★ Some scientists believe that colors cause certain feelings in people. Blues and greens are called "cool" colors and are thought to be relaxing. Reds and yellows are known as "hot" colors because they are believed to stimulate the brain. In fact, red in bedrooms might cause restlessness and insomnia.

★ Cats are thought to be color-blind, while monkeys, apes, and birds have color vision similar to humans.

★ Bees have color vision and can also detect ultraviolet wavelengths that are too short for humans to see. In fact, some flowers reflect ultraviolet light to attract bees. (Figure 12-4)

Bees can see colors.

Figure 12-4

Ask some grown-ups this question.
Bet they don't know!

WHY IS THE SKY BLUE?

YOUR CHALLENGE

To scatter light and produce colors like the sky.

DO THIS

1   Use the pencil to make a hole in the center of one end of the box. Use the scissors to cut the hole about 1 inch (2.54 cm) in diameter.

2   Stand the sheet of paper in the opposite end of the box. (It's okay if the paper curves around the sides of the box.) Place the box in a sunny area with the side of the box facing the sun. This position will keep sunlight from entering the box through the hole. If no sunlight is available, place the box in a darkened room and use a flashlight.

3   Next, put the glass of water in the center of the box about halfway between the hole and the white paper.

YOU NEED

Pencil

Cardboard box (shoe box)

Scissors

Sheet of white paper

Mirror and sunny day

Flashlight and darkened room (if no sunlight available)

Clear glass of water

Small amount of milk

53

4 Use the mirror to reflect a beam of sunlight through the hole, through the glass of water, and onto the white paper. Notice the color of the light beam as it passes through the glass of water. What color is the spot of light on the paper? (Figure 13-1)

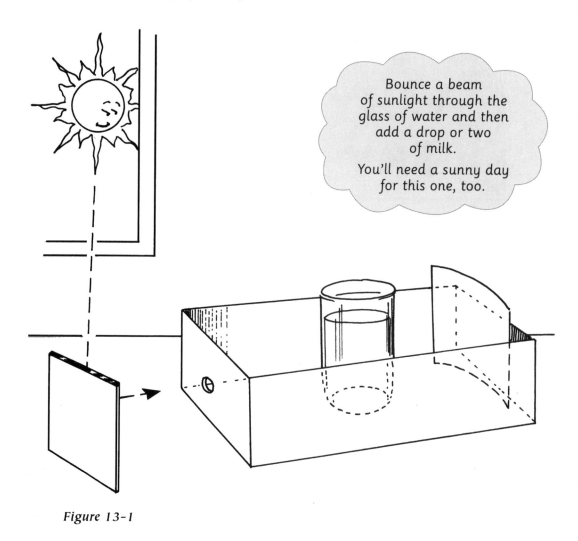

Bounce a beam of sunlight through the glass of water and then add a drop or two of milk.

You'll need a sunny day for this one, too.

Figure 13-1

5 Now drop a single drop of milk into the water and stir the solution. Shine the light through the hole again and notice the color of the beam. Add another drop of milk to the water and repeat the steps.

WHAT HAPPENED?

When light was shined through the hole, it became a narrow beam, passed through the glass of clear water, then made a white spot on the paper. When one drop of milk was added to the water, the beam turned gray with a faint tinge of blue as it entered the glass. As the light traveled through more of the solution, it took on an orange tint and produced an orange spot on the paper. With the second drop of milk, the spot on the paper turned more orange, like our sun at sunrise. The added milk represents our atmosphere.

Light from the sun is made up of different colors that become visible when the beams of light are bent. As light from the sun passes through the atmosphere, it is scattered by air molecules, by dust particles, and by molecules of water vapor. The atmosphere scatters blue light, but not the other colors. This makes the sky appear blue. (Figure 13-2)

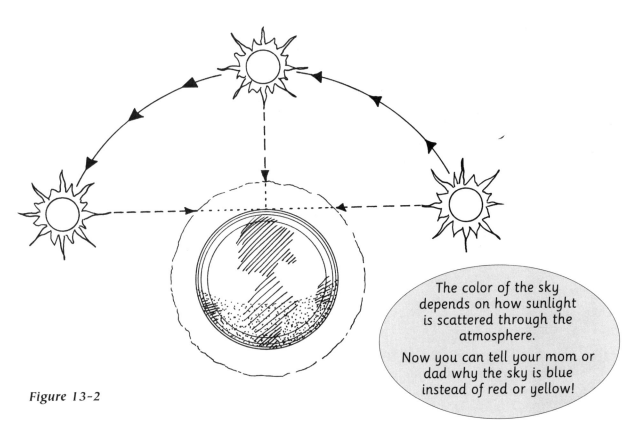

Figure 13-2

The color of the sky depends on how sunlight is scattered through the atmosphere.

Now you can tell your mom or dad why the sky is blue instead of red or yellow!

When sunlight strikes the earth at an angle, it must pass through more of the atmosphere than when it is directly overhead. Dust and other particles in the air allow only the red light to get through. This makes the sun appear red at sunrise and sunset.

What does the saying, "Red sun in the morning, sailors take warning; red sun at night, sailors' delight," mean? How could this be used to predict the weather? What is the color of the sky in space? Why is it that color?

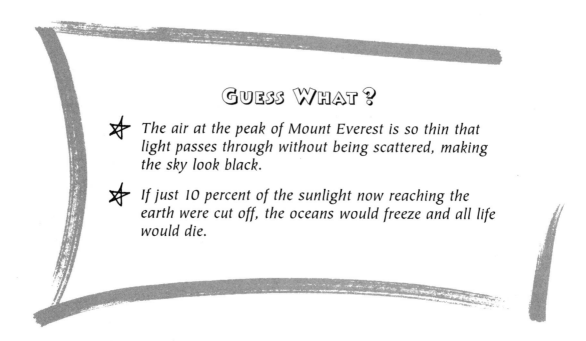

GUESS WHAT?

⭐ *The air at the peak of Mount Everest is so thin that light passes through without being scattered, making the sky look black.*

⭐ *If just 10 percent of the sunlight now reaching the earth were cut off, the oceans would freeze and all life would die.*

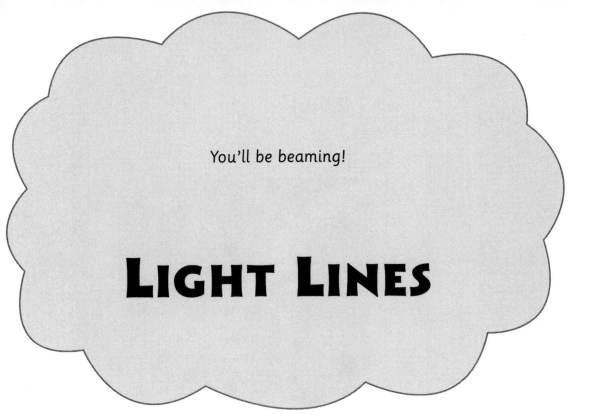

You'll be beaming!

LIGHT LINES

YOUR CHALLENGE

To observe light traveling in a straight line.

DO THIS

1   Using the pencil, make a small hole in the center of the black paper.

2   Place the paper over a sunlit window and darken the room as much as possible. (Figure 14-1)

3   Look at the light coming through the hole. If the beam of light cannot be seen clearly, sprinkle some baby powder or flour in the air above the beam. (Figure 14-2)

YOU NEED

Large sheet of black construction paper

Pencil

Sunlit window

Baby powder or flour

Tape a sheet of
black paper
over a window.

The idea is to have
most of the sunlight
blocked out,
except what is
coming through
the hole.

Figure 14-1

WHAT HAPPENED?

Describe what you see. How would the light look if it was not traveling in a straight line?

Early theories evolved on how light travels. Some scientists thought that light traveled in a stream of tiny particles, while others believed it traveled in waves. Later, it was discovered that light itself is an electromagnetic disturbance in the form of waves. This meant that light was both electrical and magnetic. In 1900, the idea was established that light is made up of little packages of energy called *quanta*.

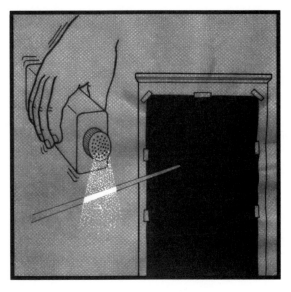

Sprinkle
baby powder
or flour
to see
the beam
more clearly.

Figure 14-2

Since light is an electric and magnetic disturbance, how do sunspots
(dark patches on the sun's surface) affect the weather on earth? What
effect could sunspots have on communications? On radio and television
transmissions? If light is an electromagnetic phenomenon (meaning that
it is both electric and magnetic), could a magnet bend a ray of light?

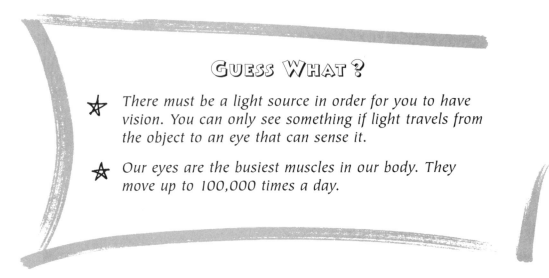

GUESS WHAT?

☆ *There must be a light source in order for you to have
vision. You can only see something if light travels from
the object to an eye that can sense it.*

☆ *Our eyes are the busiest muscles in our body. They
move up to 100,000 times a day.*

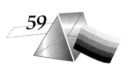

60

Whose bright idea was this experiment?

DON'T CARE FOR GLARE?

YOUR CHALLENGE

To observe how the design of lenses can reduce glare.

DO THIS

1 Place one lens over the other and look through both toward the lamp. (Figure 15-1)

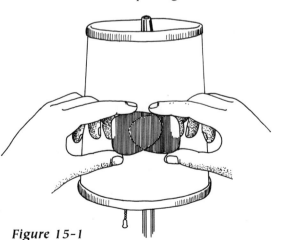

Figure 15-1

Polarized lenses have vertical lines that reduce glare.

Make sure to use an old pair of sunglasses so your parents don't freak!

61

2 Now hold one lens and slowly rotate the other. (Figure 15-2)

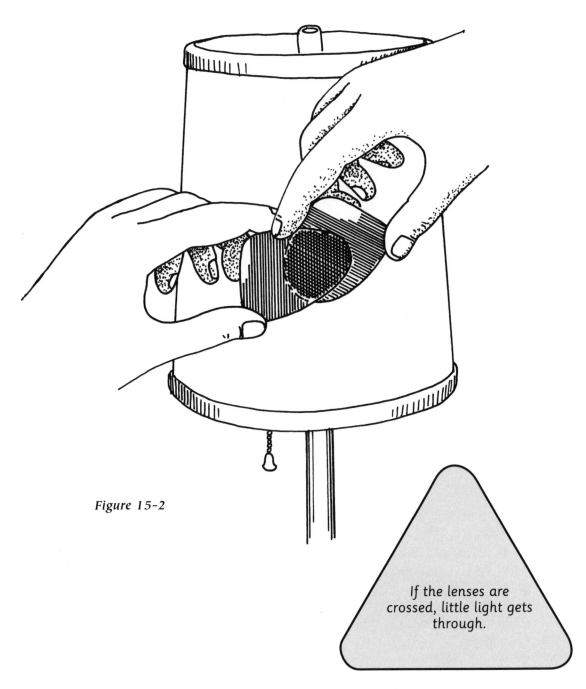

Figure 15-2

If the lenses are crossed, little light gets through.

WHAT HAPPENED?

The lenses of polarized sunglasses are made up of vertical lines. In this experiment, the lens in front *polarizes* (separates) the light waves coming through it. If the lines in the second lens are lined up with the lines in the front lens, the polarized light is able to pass through. When the second lens was rotated, though, the first lens still produced a polarized beam but was unable to pass through the second lens. This caused most of the light to be shut out.

Light traveling in waves that strike a shiny surface is reflected off, producing a glare around the object. The lines in the lenses form a grating that acts like a filter to reduce the glare.

Would a windshield that reduces glare be useful in cars? In aircraft? Why do skiers wear sunglasses? Could the glare from snow produce a sunburn? What uses can you think of for polarized light?

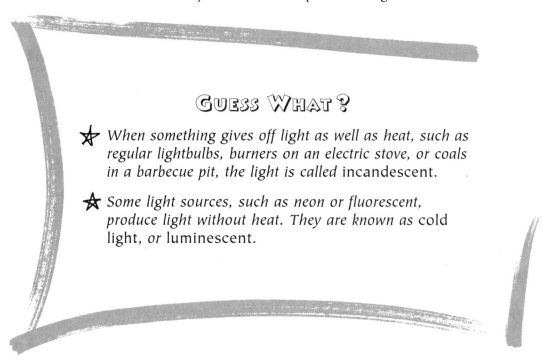

GUESS WHAT?

⭐ *When something gives off light as well as heat, such as regular lightbulbs, burners on an electric stove, or coals in a barbecue pit, the light is called* incandescent.

⭐ *Some light sources, such as neon or fluorescent, produce light without heat. They are known as* cold light, *or* luminescent.

*The colors of the rainbow
are all wet!
Get it?*

BENDING BEAMS

YOUR CHALLENGE

To observe how light refracts, or bends, as it passes through different materials.

DO THIS

1   Use the pencil and ruler to make two vertical lines in one end of the box. Draw the lines in the center about ¾ inch (2 cm) apart.

2   Use the scissors to cut each line into a slit about ⅛ inch (.3 cm) wide. (Figure 16-1)

3   Place the box in a sunny area with the side facing the sun. This will keep sunlight from entering the slits. If no sunlight is available, place the box in a darkened room and use a flashlight.

YOU NEED

Cardboard box

Pencil

Ruler

Scissors

Mirror and sunlight

Flashlight and darkened room (if no sunlight available)

Clear glass of water

Two sheets of white paper

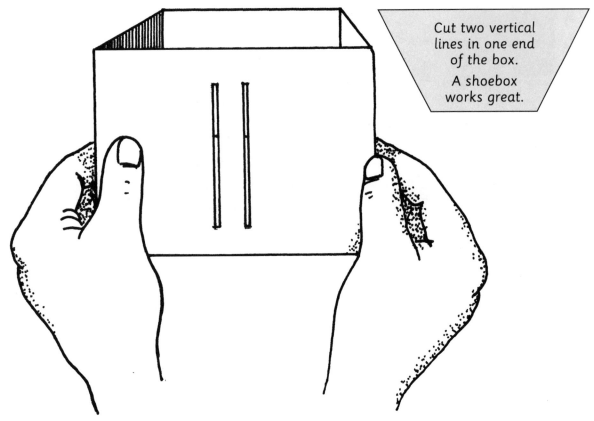

Figure 16-1

4   Once the box is in position, place a sheet of paper in the bottom of the box, and the other paper at the end opposite the two slits. It is okay if this sheet curves around the sides of the box.

5   Now place the glass of water in the center of the box about halfway between the slits and the white paper.

6   Use the mirror or flashlight to shine a beam of light through the slits, through the glass of water, and onto the paper. Adjust the beams of light until you can see them across the bottom of the box. (Figure 16-2)

Reflect a beam of light through the slits in the box.

You'll need to play around with the mirror to get the angle just right.

Figure 16-2

WHAT HAPPENED?

When you shined the light through the slits, it formed two parallel beams, entered the curved sides of the glass, and came out at an angle. The beams were bent, or *refracted*, because they struck the glass at an angle. If the glass had been flat, the beams would not have bent.

67

The beams then passed through the other side of the glass, crossed, and produced two vertical white lines on the paper. If the beams were adjusted just right, you probably noticed that they were much brighter where they crossed. At this point, the beams combined at a point to produce the extra brightness. (Figure 16-3)

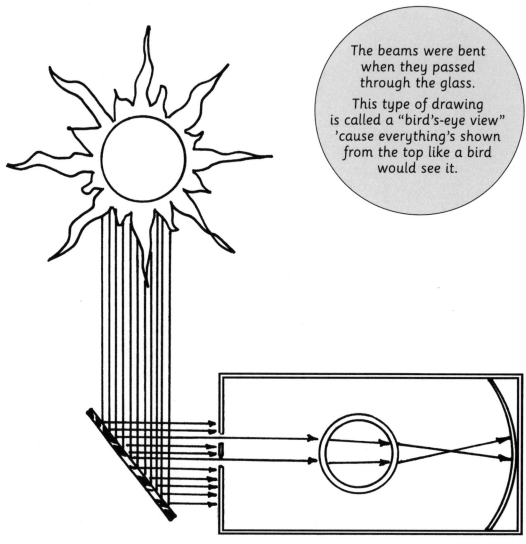

The beams were bent when they passed through the glass.

This type of drawing is called a "bird's-eye view" 'cause everything's shown from the top like a bird would see it.

Figure 16-3

What uses can you think of for bending light? Would this ability be beneficial in medicine? How could the extra brightness where the beams crossed be useful? Could it generate heat? How do raindrops bend sunlight, and what effect can this produce?

GUESS WHAT ?

★ *Rainbows appear when the sun's rays are reflected in particles of water, or raindrops, in the sky. Sometimes two rainbows form at the same time, one inside the other. When this happens, the order of the colors of one rainbow is opposite the order of colors of the other rainbow. This happens because sunlight is reflected twice inside each raindrop.*

★ *Plants need the sun to change light into food out of air and minerals. The process is called* photosynthesis.

Hot air is no mirage—
you can see it move!

SHAKY SHADOWS

YOUR CHALLENGE

To bend light by passing it through different densities of air.

DO THIS

 1 Before starting the experiment, tie up loose hair or clothing that could come in contact with the flame. Always be extra careful when working with fire.

 2 Place the lighted candle on the table so that the candle is about 2 feet (61 cm) from a light-colored wall or a sheet of white paper.

3 Turn the room's lights off. Shine the flashlight through the space above the candle to cast a shadow on the wall. (Figure 17-1)

YOU NEED

Lighted candle

Table

Light-colored wall or sheet of white paper

Darkened room

Flashlight

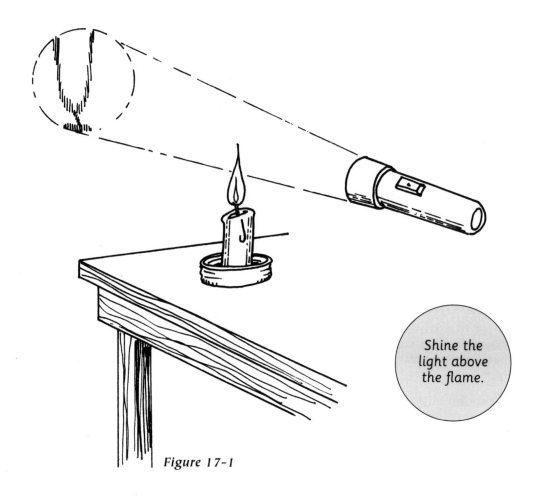

Shine the
light above
the flame.

Figure 17-1

What Happened?

You should see flickering shadows on the wall rising from the flame of
the candle. When air is heated, it expands and becomes less dense than
the surrounding air. The thinner air causes the light to bend slightly,
creating a faint shadow. Any disturbance, such as a baseball traveling
through the air, will cause the air to press together into waves. These air
waves are compacted and more dense than the surrounding air. The
different densities of the air will cause the light passing through to form
shadow pictures.

Refracting, or bending, of light on a hot day can create the illusion of a distant pool of water on pavement. Light from the sun is bent as it passes through the rising hot air near the pavement and creates what appears to be a shiny pool of water. It is not really water, but an illusion created by light that is bent as it passes through the different densities of the rising air near the surface.

Shadow pictures are very useful. For example, engineers study shadow pictures of high-speed aircraft and rockets to create more efficient designs. Waves from a boat moving through the water make similar patterns. What other uses can you think of for shadow pictures? Could they help in the design of more fuel-efficient cars?

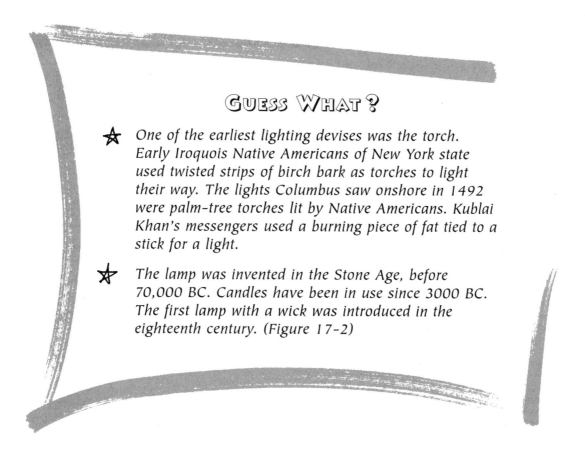

GUESS WHAT?

★ *One of the earliest lighting devises was the torch. Early Iroquois Native Americans of New York state used twisted strips of birch bark as torches to light their way. The lights Columbus saw onshore in 1492 were palm-tree torches lit by Native Americans. Kublai Khan's messengers used a burning piece of fat tied to a stick for a light.*

★ *The lamp was invented in the Stone Age, before 70,000 BC. Candles have been in use since 3000 BC. The first lamp with a wick was introduced in the eighteenth century. (Figure 17-2)*

Early forms of lighting.
Is this what they meant
by the dark ages?

Figure 17-2

Will the last person leaving the universe
please turn out the lights?

DIFFRACTION ACTION

YOUR CHALLENGE

To bend light around the edges of a smooth surface.

DO THIS

1 Attach one end of the thread to the marble with glue.

2 While the glue is drying, place the box on the floor,
   underneath a table. Place the flashlight on top of the box
   so that its beam shines out into the room.

3 Suspend the marble from the edge of the table so that it
   is about 3 inches (7.62 cm) in front of, and exactly in line
   with, the beam from the flashlight. Secure the thread to
   the table with a small strip of tape.

4 When the suspended marble is still, place the white
   paper directly behind the marble to form a dark,
   sharp shadow. (Figure 18-1)

YOU NEED

Thread

Dark-colored marble

Glue

Table

**Large box to use as
support for flashlight**

Flashlight

**Transparent tape or
masking tape**

Piece of white paper

75

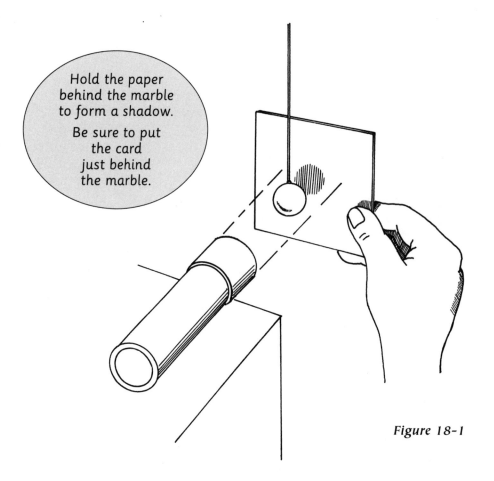

Hold the paper behind the marble to form a shadow.

Be sure to put the card just behind the marble.

Figure 18-1

5   Now slowly move the paper away, gradually reducing the size of the shadow until it becomes a dark spot. (Figure 18-2)

6   Continue moving the paper back. (Figure 18-3)

WHAT HAPPENED?

The dark spot will suddenly turn into a bright white spot in the middle of a grayish shadow. This is called the *Arago white spot,* named after the French scientist, Dominique Arago, who discovered it.

The light waves are diffracted as they pass the edge of the marble. The light bends around the marble to form a white spot in its shadow. The

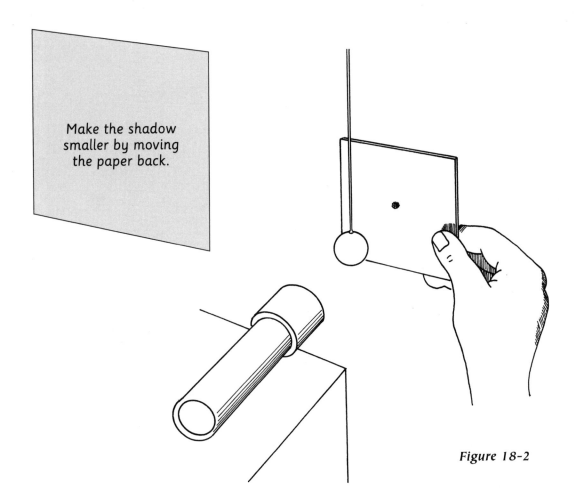

Make the shadow smaller by moving the paper back.

Figure 18-2

center of the shadow is the focusing point for the light from the edge of the marble. The rest of the area of the shadow is darker because the light waves arriving there are diffracted differently and are traveling different distances. They interfere with each other and are not in focus.

If light bends slightly, how could this be a problem for astronomers? Bring your thumb and forefinger almost together and look through the gap at a light source. Can you see a shadow forming just before your finger touches your thumb? Are the light rays bending and forming the shadow?

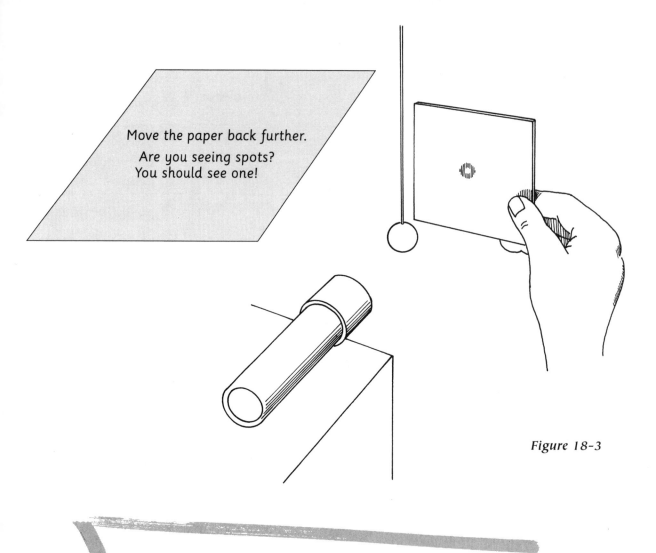

Move the paper back further.

Are you seeing spots?
You should see one!

Figure 18-3

You have to look below the surface
to find the answer!

THE INVISIBLE
PENCIL

YOUR CHALLENGE

To observe the mirrored effect of water.

DO THIS

1   Place the pencil in an empty glass and look at it through
    the side of the glass. (Figure 19-1)

2   Remove the pencil and fill the glass about three-fourths
    full of water.

3   Lower the pencil into the glass and look at it again
    through the side. What happens?

4   Hold the glass at arm's length in front of you, slightly
    above your head. Look up at the pencil and the area
    below the surface of the water. (Figure 19-2)

YOU NEED

Pencil
Clear drinking glass
Water

Place a pencil in a glass.

You'll bend the rules of optics with this one!

Figure 19-1

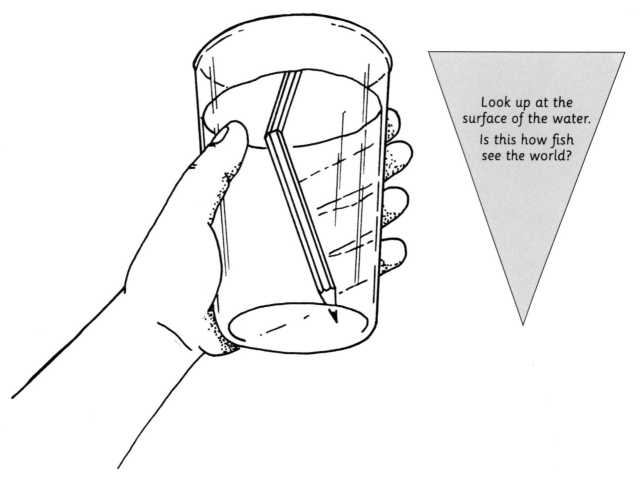

Look up at the surface of the water.

Is this how fish see the world?

Figure 19-2

WHAT HAPPENED?

The pencil and nothing else can be seen above the water. If you look at the surface at an angle from below, the surface acts like a mirror. The light rays are reflected back. If you hold the glass straight overhead, the mirror effect goes away. The light rays are not reflected back.

If you shined a flashlight at an angle from below the surface of smooth water, would the light bounce back? Could someone above the surface see the light? What results would you get if you repeated the experiment in the dark?

GUESS WHAT?

⭐ *Bright sunlight reflected from water can cause a sunburn.*

⭐ *Nothing travels faster than light.*

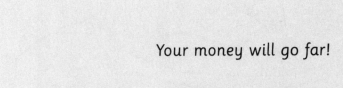

Your money will go far!

MOVING MONEY

YOUR CHALLENGE

To bend light and observe the image it produces.

DO THIS

1 Place the coin in the bowl at the edge where the bowl starts to slope upward. This will be a reference point. (Figure 20-1)

2 Look at the coin from an angle above the lip of the bowl. Position your head so that you can only see the outer edge of the coin. (Figure 20-2)

3 Keep looking at the coin, and very slowly pour water into the bowl. (Figure 20-3)

YOU NEED

Cereal bowl

Coin (nickel or quarter)

Container of water

83

Figure 20-1

Place a coin at the
edge of the bowl.

Make sure it's
all the way to
the edge.

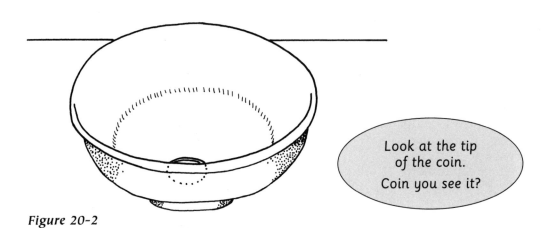

Look at the tip
of the coin.

Coin you see it?

Figure 20-2

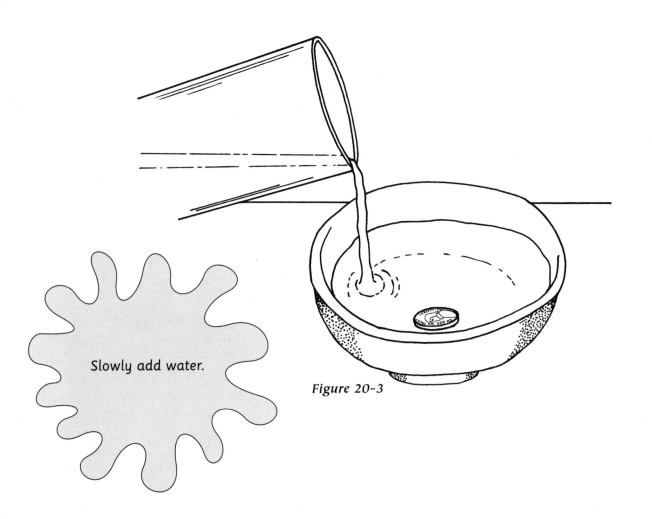

Slowly add water.

Figure 20-3

WHAT HAPPENED?

The coin will appear to move toward the center of the bowl until it is in full view. Make sure that the coin hasn't moved by looking at the reference point.

When there was no water in the bowl, the light traveled in a straight line from the coin to your eyes. As you looked over the edge of the bowl, only the outer edge of the coin was reflecting light to your eyes. When water was added to the bowl, the light rays were bent, or refracted, by the water. The angle of the bending was great enough to allow all of the light reflected from the coin to travel to your eyes.

85

Are objects in water where they appear to be? How would you adjust your aim if you were spearfishing? Is this a form of optical illusion?

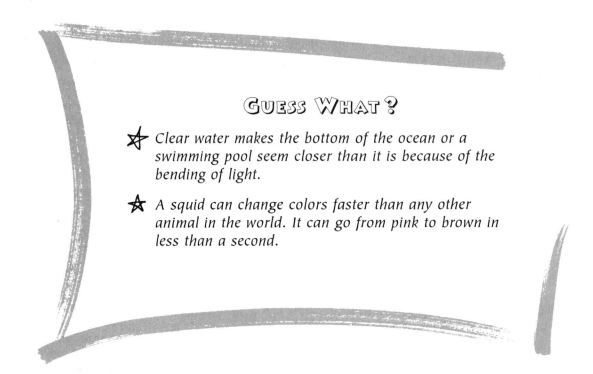

GUESS WHAT?

⭐ *Clear water makes the bottom of the ocean or a swimming pool seem closer than it is because of the bending of light.*

⭐ *A squid can change colors faster than any other animal in the world. It can go from pink to brown in less than a second.*

Don't be a drip—this one's fun!

Dark Spots from Clear Water

Your Challenge

To observe how light rays are affected by a drop of water.

Do This

 1 Place the piece of glass on a sheet of white paper. (Be careful with the glass. Its edges could be sharp!)

2 Place a few drops of water about a ½-inch diameter (1.3 cm) on the glass. (Figure 21-1)

3 Hold the glass in the sunlight so that the spots cast their shadow on the white paper. Raise and lower the glass to the paper. (Figure 21-2)

Piece of glass (for example, from a picture frame)

Sheet of white paper

Drops of water

Sunlight or flashlight

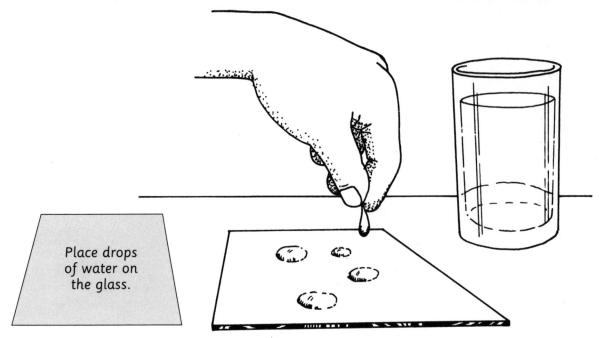

Place drops
of water on
the glass.

Figure 21-1

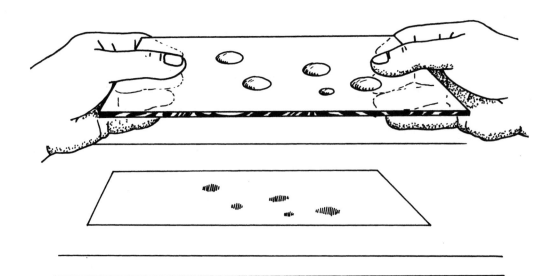

Figure 21-2

Raise and lower the glass.
Careful with the edges!

WHAT HAPPENED?

When the glass is next to the paper, the drops act like magnifying lenses, and you see a clear spot below them. As the glass is raised, the bright spot grows smaller and is surrounded by a very dark ring.

The light rays striking the glass pass through evenly, but the rays striking the rounded drops of water are bent as they pass through the water. When the rays hit the paper, most of the light can be concentrated in an area of bright light, but the remaining light rays are distorted and make up the dark area.

What happens to light rays as they pass through raindrops? Are raindrops round or tear-shaped? How do dust particles or pollution in rain affect light rays?

GUESS WHAT?

⭐ *Light travels slower through water than through air.*

⭐ *The sun's surface temperature is about 10,300°F (5,700°C).*

You have to stand on your head
and read backwards
to get this experiment!

HOME MOVIES

YOUR CHALLENGE

To project an image onto a "screen."

DO THIS

1   Turn on the lamp and turn off the room lights.

2   Hold the magnifying glass level, about 10 inches
    (25 cm) above the lightbulb. Raise and lower the
    magnifying glass until you have a sharp image on the
    ceiling. (Figure 22-1)

WHAT HAPPENED ?

When you got the image in focus, the printing and numbers
that were projected on the ceiling appeared large and clear,
except they were upside down and backwards. The effect is
similar to a slide show. The bulb was the source of light, the
printing took the place of the slide, and the ceiling became

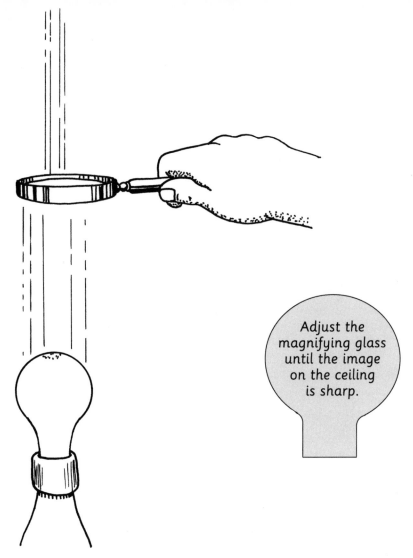

Figure 22-1

the screen. The magnifying glass was raised or lowered until it brought the printing to a focal point based on the distance from the printing to the ceiling. A *focal point* is where light beams converge to bring an image into focus.

Why do you think the image was reversed? What happened to the light as it passed through the magnifying glass? How could you reverse the image so that it reads correctly? What effect would two magnifying glasses have on the image?

GUESS WHAT?

⭐ *The first projector, called a* camera obscura, *was a darkened room with a single, small opening on an outside wall. The image of an illuminated object on the outside traveled through the hole and was projected upside down on the opposite wall. Later, a lightproof box with a lens inserted in the hole produced the same results.*

⭐ *In 1826, French inventor Joseph N. Niepce used this principle to project an image onto light-sensitive paper and became the first person to take a picture.*

⭐ *Niepce's first photograph required an exposure time of about 8 hours.*

You'll be head over heels!

FLIPPING OUT

YOUR CHALLENGE

To observe the principles of the first cameras.

DO THIS

 1   Carefully cut a 2-inch-square (5 cm) opening in the center of the bottom of the box. Never cut with the object held against yourself. You could slip and seriously injure yourself! (Figure 23-1)

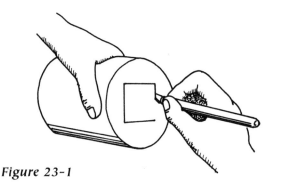

Cut a square in the box.

Figure 23-1

YOU NEED

Round oatmeal box with lid

Utility knife

Piece of wax paper about 3 inches (8 cm) square

Masking tape

Piece of aluminum foil about 2 inches (5 cm) square

Needle

Darkened room

Small table lamp with the shade removed

2   Tape the wax paper over this opening. This will be the viewing screen. (Figure 23-2)

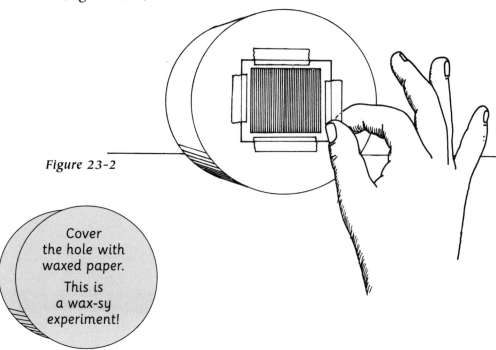

Figure 23-2

Cover
the hole with
waxed paper.

This is
a wax-sy
experiment!

3   Cut a 1-inch-square (2.5 cm) opening in the center of the lid. Tape the aluminum foil over this opening. (Figure 23-3)

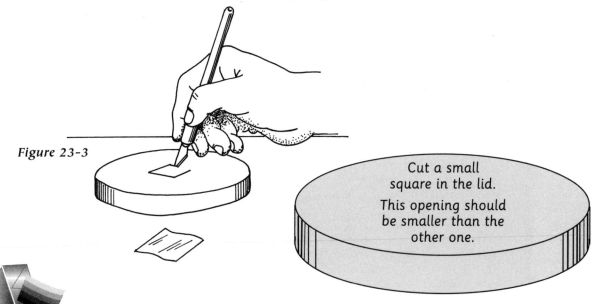

Figure 23-3

Cut a small
square in the lid.

This opening should
be smaller than the
other one.

4 Using the needle, make a small opening in the center of the aluminum foil. This is where the lines of light will cross. Put the lid back on the box. (Figure 23-4)

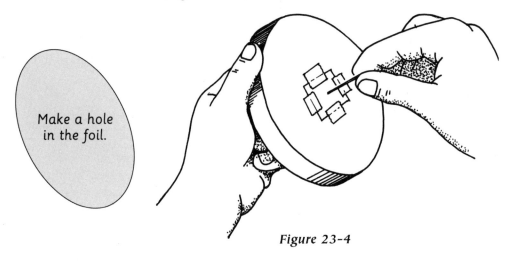

Make a hole in the foil.

Figure 23-4

5 In a darkened room, turn the lamp on.

6 Aim the end of the box with the pinhole at the lightbulb. Hold the box about 4 inches (10 cm) from the bulb, and slowly move it back and forth until a clear image appears on the wax paper. (Figure 23-5)

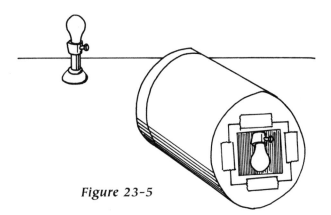

Figure 23-5

An image will appear on the paper.

WHAT HAPPENED?

The image will be sharp, but it will be upside down because light travels in a straight line through the pinhole. This happens because the light traveling from the top of the lamp travels through the pinhole and strikes the bottom of the wax paper, while light from the bottom of the lamp travels through the pinhole to the top of the wax paper. The pinhole acts as a lens, and the image is inverted.

The same thing happens in our eyes. The image is formed inverted on the back part of our eye. Our brain turns the image right-side up.

Is a photographic negative the opposite of the developed picture? The next time you get a roll of film developed, compare the negative to the photo. Did the viewfinders of old cameras show people upside down?

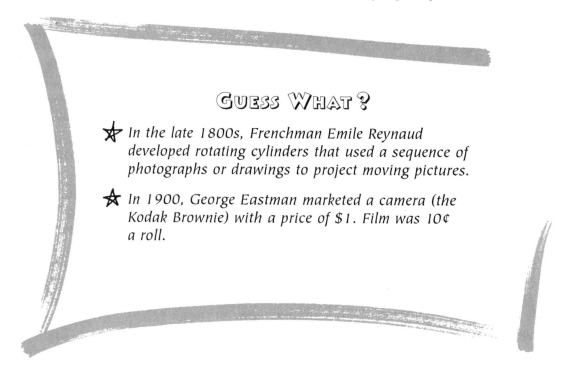

GUESS WHAT?

★ In the late 1800s, Frenchman Emile Reynaud developed rotating cylinders that used a sequence of photographs or drawings to project moving pictures.

★ In 1900, George Eastman marketed a camera (the Kodak Brownie) with a price of $1. Film was 10¢ a roll.

You'll see the big picture with this one!

LIQUID LENS

YOUR CHALLENGE

To use water to magnify an image.

DO THIS

1   Bend a round loop about ¼ inch (6mm) in diameter in one end of the wire. To do this, use the pointed end of a pencil as a guide, wrap the wire around the pencil, and twist the wire together. (Figure 24-1)

2   Dip the wire loop in the bowl of water and slowly remove it. Water will stay inside the loop. This is the lens. (Figure 24-2)

3   Look through the lens at a printed page or examine the texture of a piece of fabric. (Figure 24-3)

YOU NEED

Piece of fine wire, about 6 inches (15 cm) long

Pencil

Bowl of water

Printed page or piece of fabric

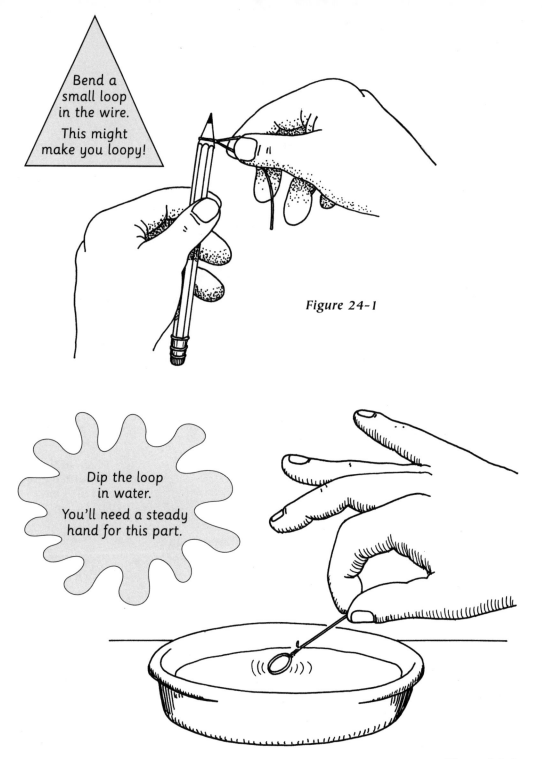

Bend a small loop in the wire.

This might make you loopy!

Figure 24-1

Dip the loop in water.

You'll need a steady hand for this part.

Figure 24-2

Figure 24-3

WHAT HAPPENED?

The circle of water acts like a magnifying lens. Most lenses are made of glass, but any transparent material can be used. In this case, both sides of the water lens curve outward and form a double convex lens. Double convex lenses are used in magnifying glasses.

Could a glass of water be used to magnify an image? Is the image reversed? Would olives look larger in a round jar than a square one?

GUESS WHAT?

★ Because it takes 8 minutes for sunlight to reach the earth, at sunrise you are really seeing the sun 8 minutes after it actually comes above the horizon. At sunset you are actually seeing it where it was 8 minutes earlier.

★ If the moon produced its own light, it would take more than 200,000 full moons to give the earth as much light as the sun does.

This project will blow
things out of proportion!

Mystifying Magnifying

Your Challenge

To invert an image with a magnifying glass.

Do This

1   Hold the sheet of paper up to the window.

2   Hold the magnifying glass about 12 inches (30.48 cm)
    from the sheet of paper. The lens should be facing toward
    the window but not in the direct sunlight.

3   Focus the lens by slowly moving it back and forth until an
    image of the window and the landscape outside appears
    on the paper. (Figure 25-1)

You Need

Sunlit window

Sheet of white paper

Magnifying glass

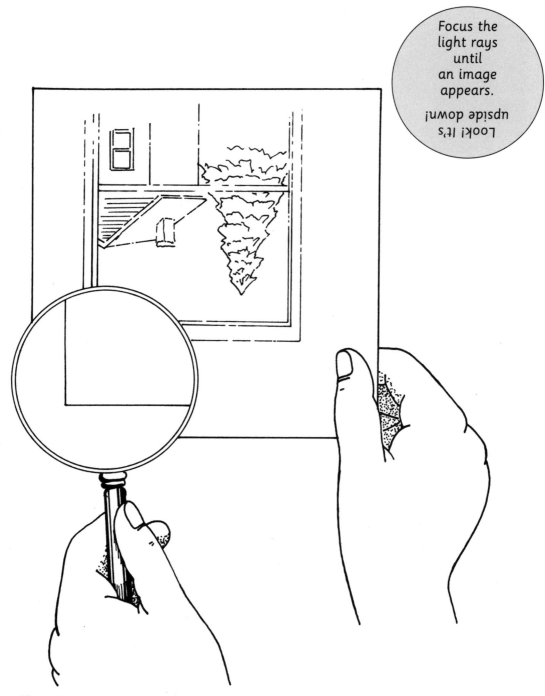

Focus the
light rays
until
an image
appears.

Look! It's
upside down!

Figure 25-1

WHAT HAPPENED?

The image will appear upside down. In this case, light rays traveling through the lens continue almost in a straight line, like the camera lens. The light from the upper part of the window creates the light for the bottom part of the image on the paper. The light from the lower part of the window produces the top part of the image.

Does your classroom have an overhead projector? How does an overhead projector work? Would it need a mirror, or prism, to transfer an image onto a wall? Would a projector be helpful to an artist, or to someone drawing blueprints? What is a hologram? Is it a type of projection?

GUESS WHAT?

★ One of the most advanced projectors can be seen in planetariums. It can project the position of stars and planets for any place in time from the earliest days of civilization on into the future.

★ Holograms are used on credit cards and even book covers.

It's a rad experiment—with light rays!

REFRACTION REACTION

YOUR CHALLENGE

To compare blocked light rays as they pass through a magnifying glass.

DO THIS

1 Tape the paper to the back of the book. Open the book so that it will stand upright on the table. Face the paper toward the window.

2 Position the magnifying glass about 12 inches (30 cm) in front of the paper, out of direct sunlight.

3 Move the magnifying glass back and forth until a full image of the window appears on the paper. After you have a sharp image, slowly pass one finger in front of the glass. Notice that the image only gets a little dimmer. (Figure 26-1)

YOU NEED

Sheet of white paper

Transparent tape

Large hardback book

Table

Sunlit window

Magnifying glass

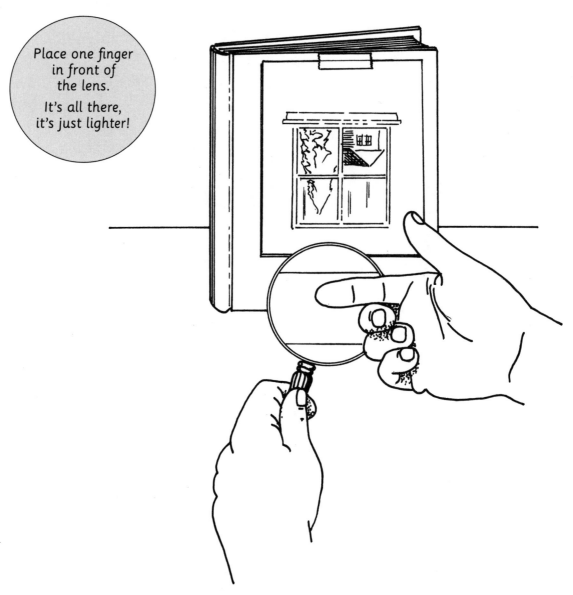

Figure 26-1

4   Now cover the top half of the lens with your hand. You would expect
    the bottom half of the image to disappear. Try covering the bottom
    half of the lens. The full image of the window still remains on the
    paper. It is only dimmer. (Figure 26-2)

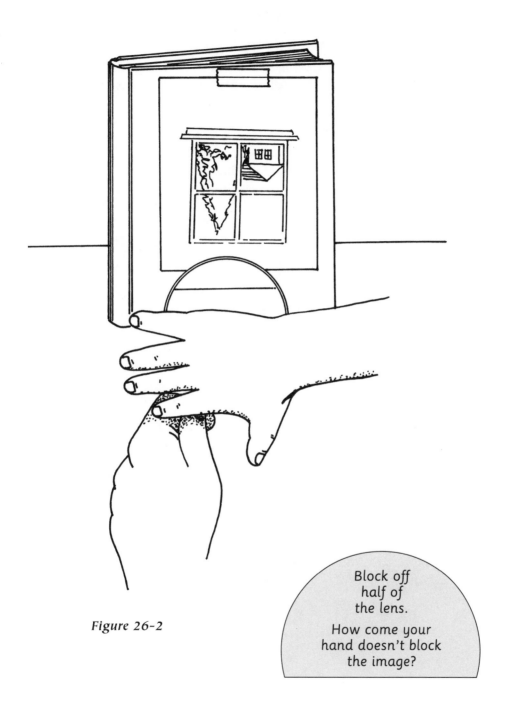

Figure 26-2

Block off
half of
the lens.

How come your
hand doesn't block
the image?

What Happened?

The light rays coming from the window and passing through the lens are refracted, or bent, from so many angles that a full image will appear. However, because half of the light was blocked off, the image was not as bright or distinct.

Can this result cause problems when using an overhead projector? How could this be useful in creating special effects?

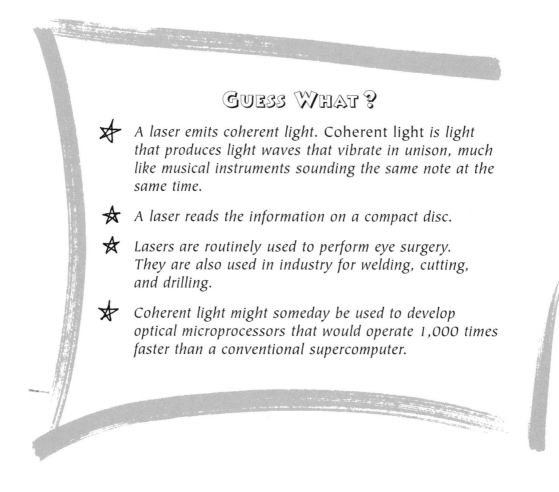

Guess What?

⭐ A laser emits coherent light. Coherent light *is light that produces light waves that vibrate in unison, much like musical instruments sounding the same note at the same time.*

⭐ *A laser reads the information on a compact disc.*

⭐ *Lasers are routinely used to perform eye surgery. They are also used in industry for welding, cutting, and drilling.*

⭐ *Coherent light might someday be used to develop optical microprocessors that would operate 1,000 times faster than a conventional supercomputer.*

Warning: Objects in this experiment are farther than they appear!

VIEWS ON VIEWING

YOUR CHALLENGE

To build a simple reflecting telescope.

DO THIS

1   Place the shaving mirror on a table by a window so that the magnifying side faces toward the moon.

2   Position the flat mirror so that it faces the shaving mirror. Adjust until you can see a reflection of the moon in the flat mirror.

3   Now look through the magnifying glass at the image of the moon in the flat mirror. It should appear much closer. (Figure 27-1)

YOU NEED

Clear, moonlit night

Curved shaving or makeup mirror

Table

Window

Flat pocket mirror

Magnifying glass

Moonlight

111

Figure 27-1

WHAT HAPPENED?

Light traveling from the moon strikes the curved surface of the shaving mirror. The light is then reflected to the small flat mirror where it is again reflected through the magnifying lens. The larger curved mirror gathers light and concentrates it on the flat mirror. The lens magnifies the image.

How can curved mirrors be used to cook food, heat water, or generate electricity? Why would this be useful in remote areas of the world?

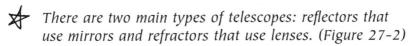

GUESS WHAT?

⭐ *There are two main types of telescopes: reflectors that use mirrors and refractors that use lenses. (Figure 27-2)*

⭐ *The 387-inch (982 cm) Keck telescope in Mauna Kea, Hawaii, is the largest in the world.*

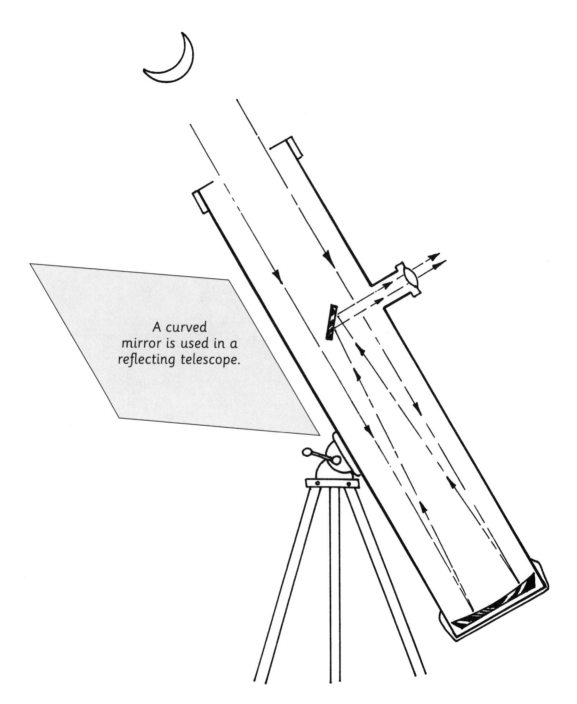

A curved mirror is used in a reflecting telescope.

Figure 27-2

*If you're not careful,
you might get dizzy!*

STROB-O-MOTION

YOUR CHALLENGE

To observe pulses of light on a moving object.

DO THIS

1 Set the compass for about a 4-inch (10 cm) radius and draw an 8-inch (20 cm) circle on the cardboard.(Figure 28-1)

 2 Keep the compass at the same setting and mark off six divisions, equally spaced, around the edge of the circle.

3 Using a ruler, draw three lines across the circle from one point to another. These will separate the circle into six equal pie-shaped parts.

4 Reduce the spread of the compass about ¼ inch (5mm) from 4 inches (10 cm) to 3¾ inches (9.5 cm). Place the point of the compass in the center of the circle, and make a small mark across each of the lines, about ¼ inch (5mm) from the edge.

YOU NEED

Compass

Ruler

Pencil

Sheet of cardboard or poster board about 8½ x 11 inches (22 x 28 cm)

Utility knife

Scissors

Phillips screwdriver

Two flat washers (to fit screwdriver)

Glue

Black marker or dull black paint

Old newspapers

Electric fan or bicycle wheel

TV

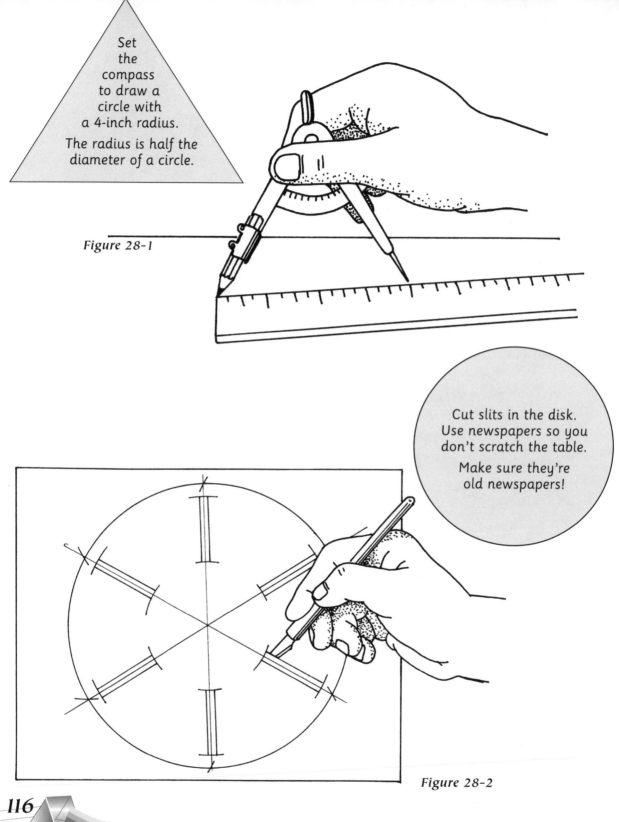

Set the compass to draw a circle with a 4-inch radius.

The radius is half the diameter of a circle.

Figure 28-1

Cut slits in the disk. Use newspapers so you don't scratch the table.

Make sure they're old newspapers!

Figure 28-2

5   Now set the compass at about 1¾ inches (4.5 cm). Keeping the point of the compass in the center of the circle, make another small mark across the lines. The two marks should be about 2 inches (5 cm) apart.

 6   Using the utility knife, carefully cut a slit between the marks, or have an adult do it. Again, never cut against yourself. Make the slit about ¼ inch (5 mm) wide and 2 inches (5 cm) long. Repeat the steps, making six slits in the circle. Then cut out the circle with the scissors. (Figure 28-2)

 7   Carefully poke the point of the screwdriver through the center of the disk to make a hole. The disk should spin freely on the shank of the screwdriver. Trim off any excess cardboard around the hole. (Figure 28-3)

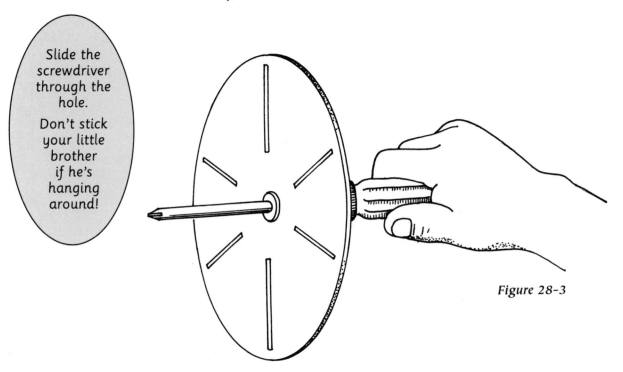

Slide the screwdriver through the hole.

Don't stick your little brother if he's hanging around!

Figure 28-3

8   Glue a flat washer to each side of the disk over the center of the hole. Make sure the washers are centered over the hole and that they are lined up with each other. Slide the screwdriver through the hole and washers as a guide before the glue sets.

9 After the glue dries, spread old newspapers on a table or countertop and use a black marker or dull black paint to cover one side of the disk.

10 After the marker or paint has dried, slide the disk onto the screwdriver with the black side facing the handle. Hold the screwdriver by the handle and point it slightly up, or at least level, so that the disk won't slide off. Raise the disk in front of your eyes and give it a spin. Look through the slits at the turning blades of an electric fan or a bicycle wheel. Try it on the TV. (Figure 28-4)

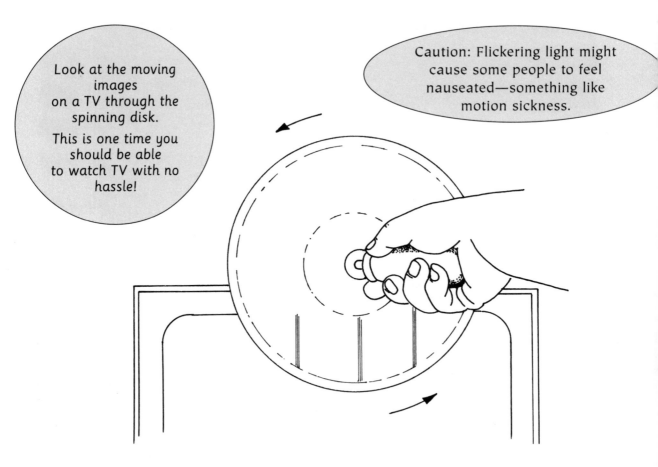

Look at the moving images
on a TV through the spinning disk.

This is one time you should be able to watch TV with no hassle!

Caution: Flickering light might cause some people to feel nauseated—something like motion sickness.

Figure 28-4

WHAT HAPPENED?

When the disk is spun at the same speed as the fan blades, the blades will appear to stand still. If the disk is spun at a slower rate, the blades will appear to turn slowly. When the disk is spun faster than the blades, the blades will seem to spin slowly, but in the wrong direction.

When you look at a TV through the spinning disk, the images appear jerky, and you can see black bars running from the upper left corner to the lower right corner of the screen. The movement appears jerky because your eyes are receiving only brief glimpses of the objects as they moved. The black bars are caused by the scanning of the electron beam as it creates the images on the screen.

The *stroboscope* is a device that uses bright pulses of light shining on a moving object to make it appear motionless or move very slowly. It allows us to study and observe things that happen at intervals too fast for the eye to see. How are stroboscopes and photography used to study and improve an athlete's performances? How could they be used in a laboratory to study mechanical devices in motion?

GUESS WHAT?

⭐ Swiftly turning fan blades appear as a blurred mass because our eyes can only see about 16 reflected light pulses per second.

⭐ Stroboscopes are used in setting the ignition timing in car engines. In this case, they are called timing lights.

⭐ Stroboscopes are also used in lighting effects for plays or concerts.

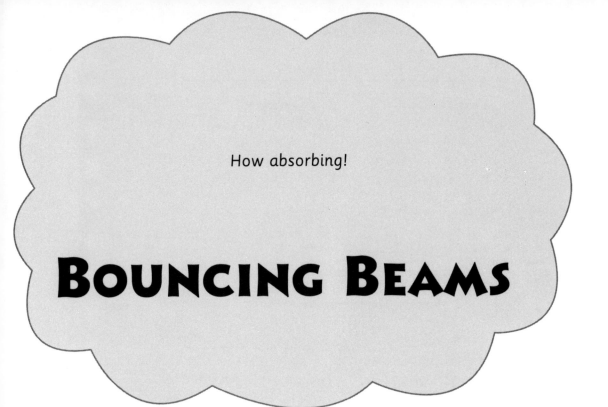

How absorbing!

BOUNCING BEAMS

YOUR CHALLENGE

To channel light through glass.

DO THIS

1   Place the dish on one of the towels. Cover the outside of the dish up to the rim with the towel. (Figure 29-1)

2   Place the other towel inside the dish, also up to the rim. This will allow any escaping light to be absorbed by the cloth. (Figure 29-2)

3   Now shine the beam of the flashlight down into the rim of the dish. Notice the opposite side of the rim. (Figure 29-3)

4   Lower one side of the towel outside the dish and shine the light through the side of the dish. Look at the rim on the opposite side of the light. How does this compare with the light being shined down into the rim?

YOU NEED

Clear glass baking dish

Two dark-colored hand towels

Flashlight

121

Place the dish on a towel.

Figure 29-1

Spread the other towel inside the dish.

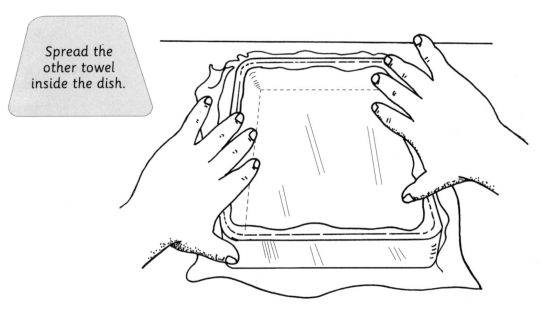

Figure 29-2

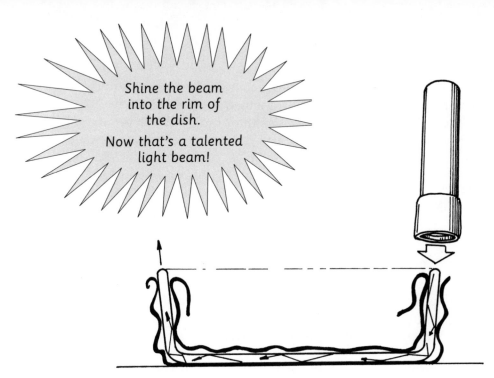

Shine the beam into the rim of the dish.

Now that's a talented light beam!

Figure 29-3

5   Now remove both towels and shine the light down into the rim of the dish as before. Look through the bottom of the dish. Is any light visible in the bottom of the dish?

WHAT HAPPENED?

When the beam of light was shined directly into the rim of the dish, it was reflected back and forth inside the glass until it came out the opposite side. When the beam was shined into the side of the glass, only a little of the light was reflected out the opposite side. Most of the light went straight through the glass.

To be channeled to the other side, the light must be shined directly into the rim, or edge, of the glass. This is the basic principle of fiber-optic technology, where light is sent into the ends of very thin glass fibers carrying information to a distant receiver. Fiber optics are used in many areas, but they have probably made the greatest impact in the field of telecommunications. In this field, fiber optics transmit sound, video, and data in the form of light pulses.

Because light travels at a much higher frequency, or level, than radio waves, do you think that the volume of transmissions would be thousands of times greater with fiber optics than radio? Why? What other uses can you think of for fiber optics?

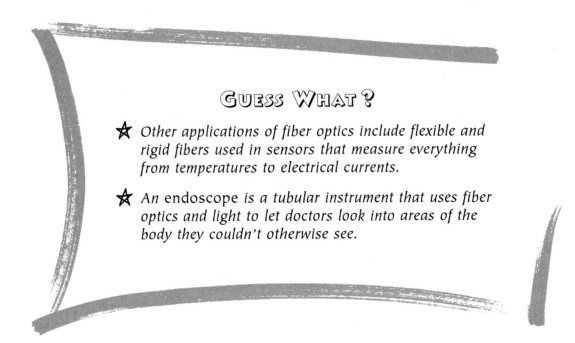

GUESS WHAT?

⭐ *Other applications of fiber optics include flexible and rigid fibers used in sensors that measure everything from temperatures to electrical currents.*

⭐ *An* endoscope *is a tubular instrument that uses fiber optics and light to let doctors look into areas of the body they couldn't otherwise see.*

Can light wave goodbye?

INSPECTING A SPECTRUM

YOUR CHALLENGE

To divide visible light into colors we can see and light we cannot see.

DO THIS

1 On a sunny morning or afternoon when the sun is about halfway above the horizon, place the pan of water in front of a window.

2 Place the mirror inside the pan so that it leans against the side of the pan. Slant the mirror at about a 45-degree angle toward the sun so that it reflects a rainbow on the wall. The pattern of colors, or *spectrum*, are the colors that make up white light. (Figure 30-1)

3 Notice the area just beyond the red band. If you had a very sensitive thermometer, you would see a temperature rise in the area even though you could see no light there.

YOU NEED

Sunlit window

Dish or pan of water

Mirror

Incandescent (regular) lamp

Fluorescent lamp

Remote control for TV (if available)

125

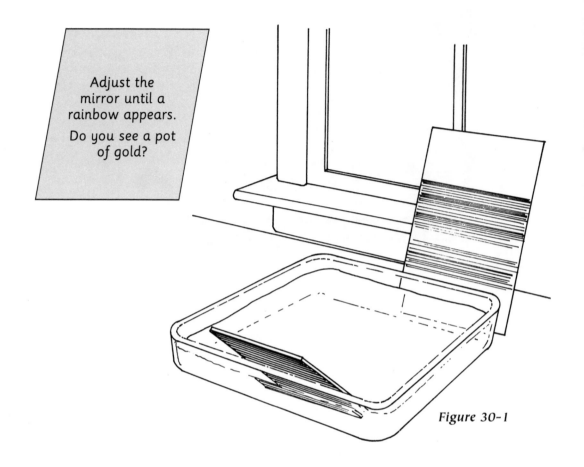

Adjust the mirror until a rainbow appears.

Do you see a pot of gold?

Figure 30-1

4   Notice the opposite end of your color spectrum, the violet band. Just past the shortest violet waves are invisible waves called *ultraviolet waves*. *Ultraviolet* means "beyond violet."

5   Turn on a regular lamp and place your hand near the bulb just close enough to feel the warmth. Now turn on a fluorescent lamp. Compare the heat from the two lamps.

6   If you have a TV with a remote control, notice that when it is used, the remote control must be aimed at a particular point on the TV.

WHAT HAPPENED?

In your experiment, the mirror in the water acted like a prism. A *prism* spreads out light waves according to their wave lengths. The shorter waves are in the violet band and the longer waves are in the red band. This means that waves that fall before the red band must be even longer. They belong to the part of the spectrum called *infrared*, or "below red." (Figure 30-2)

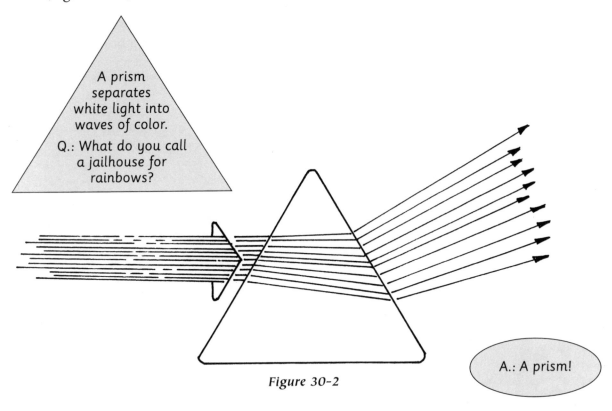

A prism separates white light into waves of color.

Q.: What do you call a jailhouse for rainbows?

A.: A prism!

Figure 30-2

The incandescent bulb in the lamp sent out waves you could see, but most of the energy was infrared, which you could only feel in the form of heat. Cameras with infrared film can take pictures in the dark because objects, including people, give off heat. Infrared cameras can locate the flames through the smoke of forest fires, allowing aircraft to pinpoint their drops. When you press the buttons of the remote control to operate a TV, the control sends out infrared radiation to a sensor in the TV.

The fluorescent lamp is a gas-filled tube with a special coating on its inner surface. When an electric current is sent through the gas, it creates *ultraviolet* waves. *Ultraviolet* means "beyond violet." They are the waves in the spectrum that fall beyond the visible violet waves. Ultraviolet waves strike the coating, causing it to glow and give off light. Ultraviolet rays from the sun can cause severe sunburns. Fortunately, the atmosphere blocks most of the sun's ultraviolet waves.

Ultraviolet radiation is sometimes called *black light,* and when it strikes certain surfaces, it causes them to glow. How would this be useful in locating some objects in the dark? Which insects glow under a black light?

The *ozone layer* is a layer of oxygen about 15 miles (24 kilometers) above the earth. It protects us from most of the ultraviolet radiation from the sun. But a hole in the ozone layer was discovered over Antarctica in 1986. Certain types of pollution cause the ozone layer to thin and in some places to disappear. What steps can we take to prevent this? Why should we?

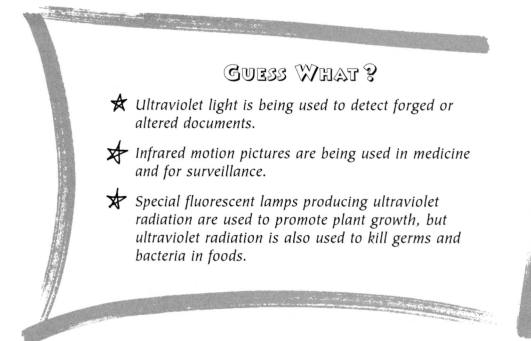

GUESS WHAT?

⭐ *Ultraviolet light is being used to detect forged or altered documents.*

⭐ *Infrared motion pictures are being used in medicine and for surveillance.*

⭐ *Special fluorescent lamps producing ultraviolet radiation are used to promote plant growth, but ultraviolet radiation is also used to kill germs and bacteria in foods.*

Brighten your day!

FUN WITH THE SUN

YOUR CHALLENGE

To use sunlight as a source of energy.

DO THIS

1 Tape black paper around one of the cans, or paint it dull black and allow it to dry. The other can should remain shiny. (Figure 31-1)

2 Fill each can with water and place a thermometer in each can.

3 Put both cans in a dark area for a few minutes. Then measure the temperature of the water inside each can.

4 Now place them in a sunny location for about the same period of time. Measure the temperature again. (Figure 31-2)

YOU NEED

Bright, sunny day

Two shiny cans about the same size (such as soup cans with labels removed)

Black construction paper or dull black paint

Water

Two thermometers

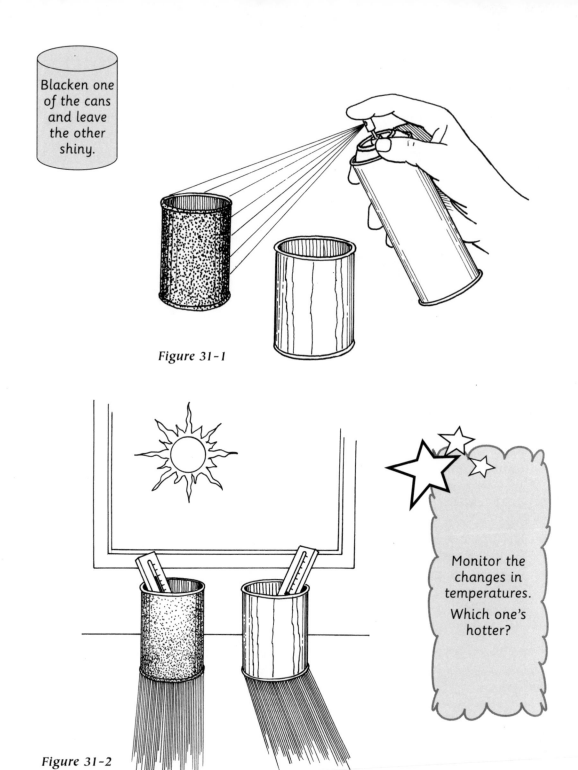

Blacken one of the cans and leave the other shiny.

Figure 31-1

Monitor the changes in temperatures.

Which one's hotter?

Figure 31-2

WHAT HAPPENED?

The temperatures inside each can were about the same after being in the dark. But after being exposed to sunlight, the water inside the darker can was much warmer than the shiny one. The dark can absorbed energy from the sun in the form of heat. The lighter one absorbed very little energy.

How can we improve the efficiency of solar collectors? Would magnifying lenses help? The common flat-plate solar collectors used to heat homes and water heaters can produce temperatures from 150° to 200°F (65° to 93°C). Can you think of some way to store this energy when the sun isn't shining? Could large rocks in an underground chamber be used?

GUESS WHAT?

★ Every day the earth receives energy from the sun that is equal to about 200,000 times the world's capacity to generate electricity. But the high cost of collecting and distributing the power has limited the use of solar energy.

★ A solar collector large enough to serve a single person for one day must have a collecting surface of about 430 square feet (40 square meters).

GLOSSARY

bioluminescence The production of light by living organisms.

coherent Sticking together or connected.

concave Hollow or curved in.

convex Curved outward like the surface of a sphere.

diffracted Light spread in a wave motion as it passes an object and expands into the area behind the object.

distort To twist out of shape or to change the normal shape or appearance of something.

erosion The process of gradually wearing away of something.

fiber optics Transparent fibers used to transmit light and images around bends and curves.

fluorescent lamp A lamp with a glass tube that is coated on the inside with a substance that gives off light.

incandescent Glowing brightly, usually from intense heat.

infrared The area containing rays just beyond the red end of the visible spectrum.

luminescent Capable of giving off low-temperature light caused by the absorption of radiant energy and not by incandescence.

Medusa One of three sisters with snakes for hair in Greek mythology.

neon A colorless and inert gaseous chemical element used in discharge tubes and gas lasers. Neon ionizes and glows red when an electric current is sent through it and is often found in advertising signs.

opaque Not letting light pass through it.

ozone layer The atmospheric layer within the stratosphere that prevents some heat loss from the earth and absorbs much of the ultraviolet radiation from the sun.

photosynthesis The process plants use to produce food, mostly sugars, from sunlight.

polarized light Light in which the motion or the field of the waves is confined to one plane or direction.

prism A transparent body, such as glass, used for refracting or dispersing light into the spectrum.

Pyrenees The mountain range along the border between France and Spain.

reflected Thrown or bounced back; used when referring to light, heat, or sound.

refraction The bending of light rays as they pass through one material to another of different densities.

spectrum The series of colored bands arranged in the order of their wavelengths by passing white light through a prism.

stroboscope An instrument for studying motion; a device that uses a rapid flashing light that illuminates a moving object.

translucent Letting light pass but diffusing it so that objects on the other side cannot be seen clearly. Frosted glass, for instance, is *translucent*.

transparent Transmitting light rays so that objects on the other side can be clearly seen.

ultraviolet The band of light waves that are just beyond the violet end of the visible spectrum.

INDEX

About the Guy Who Wrote This Book

A keen observer of nature and an avid follower of scientific advances, author Robert W. Wood injects his own special brand of fun into children's physics. His *Physics for Kids* series has been through 13 printings, and he has written more than a dozen other science books. His innovative work has been featured in major newspapers and magazines.